STRAYAPEDIA

STRAYAPEDIA

STRAYAPEDIA

The 100% fair dinkum guide to the
world's least un-Australian country

Dominic Knight

ALLEN&UNWIN
SYDNEY·MELBOURNE·AUCKLAND·LONDON

First published in 2017

Copyright © Dominic Knight 2017

Allen & Unwin
83 Alexander Street
Crows Nest NSW 2065
Australia
Phone: (61 2) 8425 0100
Email: info@allenandunwin.com
Web: www.allenandunwin.com

Cataloguing-in-Publication details are available
from the National Library of Australia
www.trove.nla.gov.au

ISBN 978 1 76029 607 0

Set in 10/18 pt Helvetica by Bookhouse, Sydney
Printed and bound in Australia by Griffin Press

10 9 8 7 6 5 4 3 2

MIX
Paper from
responsible sources
FSC® C009448

The paper in this book is FSC® certified. FSC® promotes environmentally responsible, socially beneficial and economically viable management of the world's forests.

For Divya, my favourite un-Australian

Legal disclaimer

This is a work of fiction. While the book contains entries about well-known subjects and people, none of them is intended to be taken as true in any way whatsoever. Any 'facts' cited are, in fact, alternative facts. The reader may happen to have heard that certain events mentioned herein did indeed take place—if so, this is mere coincidence.

This book is based on the Wikipedia entry for each subject that it covers—indeed, no other source has been used, because the author of this book is lazy. He has made every effort not to plagiarise Wikipedia, however, by rewriting each entry approximately as much as he rewrote his essay sources at university, and, besides, it's Creative Commons, which he thinks means that it's okay to steal.* Plus there's that whole fair dealing for parody and satire provision in Australian copyright law, which he thinks means he's allowed to do this, and he would very much appreciate you not suing him if he isn't.

However, anyone who rewrites part of this book and tries to onsell that work will be sued with the merciless fury of Donald Trump on Twitter.

In recognition of its invaluable contribution to this parody of it, a portion of the proceeds from this book will be donated to the Wikimedia Foundation to support Wikipedia, the second-greatest achievement in the history of the internet after cat memes.

---

* This is intended as a joke. Hereafter, it will not always be clear whether something is intended as a joke, which is also intentional.

Tony Abbott

Anthony John 'Tony' Abbott (born 4 November 1957, where he still resides today) was the 28th prime minister of Australia. It is also believed that he will be the next prime minister, though almost exclusively by him.

While Abbott held the role for a mere one year and 362 days, most who lived through the period felt that it lasted an eternity.

Tony Abbott on the day he took official possession of the Lodge's wine cellar. *Department of Foreign Affairs and Trade website— www.dfat.gov.au*

Abbott's key achievements as prime minister consisted of undoing the achievements of earlier prime ministers. He failed to pass a budget after two attempts, failed to pass his signature parental leave package, and failed to pass both Kevin Rudd's and Julia Gillard's total number of days in office. Upon being deposed, he promised that there would be 'no wrecking, no undermining and no sniping', another undertaking that he failed to deliver.

Abbott has the unique distinction of being the only prime minister in Australian history to be dumped within two years of winning an election. All those who served shorter terms were appointed following extraordinary circumstances, making him the most rapidly discarded elected leader in the 116 years since Australia's Federation. This lack of endurance is certain to be his most enduring accomplishment as PM, as his successor and colleague, Malcolm Turnbull, rapidly undid just about everything else.

Early life and family

Tony Abbott was born in London to an Australian mother and a British father—or, as he saw it, two British parents. In 1960, the Abbotts, along with their young son, Anthony, left the UK on the SS *Oronsay* as part of the Assisted Passage Migration Scheme. It was this formative experience of being torn from the bosom of Mother England that caused Abbott's lifelong opposition to migration by boats, given that one had been used to banish him to the opposite side of the world from the Royal Family.

The young Abbott was educated at St Ignatius' College in Sydney, a Jesuit school where he was taught to apply the Ignatian ideal of being a 'man for others'. As it was a wealthy, exclusive private school, he learned that the best way of achieving that ideal was by helping prominent business leaders become as successful as possible—as scholars have pointed out, Ignatius never specified exactly which 'others' his followers were supposed to help, so the adult Abbott concluded that Rupert Murdoch and Gina Rinehart qualified.

After school, Abbott attended the University of Sydney, where he undertook a Bachelor of Economics and a Bachelor of Laws degree. Both of these are ideal preparation for a leader trying to pass ambitious reforms to fix Australia's economy, but in this case were not.

Abbott's boxing prowess was also legendary, and he landed many successful blows on his opponents in the ring. He also landed a notorious hit on a wall in close proximity to a female political opponent.*

The future prime minister was a resident of St John's, then the university's Catholic men's college. This highly traditional and blokey environment made it easier for the young Abbott to avoid anything more than fleeting interactions with the opposite sex, and when it came time for him to consider including women in his cabinets, his college years proved formative.

Unusually for an avowed Young Liberal, Abbott's political hero was Bob Santamaria of the Democratic Labor Party, an organisation that had split from Labor to prevent what it saw as its ties with communism. Influenced by his mentor, Abbott would go on to split Labor between Rudd and Gillard.

Abbott attended Oxford on a Rhodes Scholarship, winning a blue for boxing. This was his primary preparation for his political career, in which he developed a unique style of all-out attack, without any plan for what to do after a knockout had been achieved. The young Abbott attended a seminary after university, following what he at one point believed to be inseminary activities during his time as a student.

Liberal leader

After then-leader Malcolm Turnbull supported the Rudd government's emissions trading scheme, Tony Abbott successfully harnessed the raging

---

* Although Abbott denied in parliament that this ever happened, the woman, Barbara Ramjan, has threatened legal action against several people who denied that this ever happened, and provided a sworn affidavit. Oh, to have been a fly on—well, not that wall, as it may have proven fatal—but a nearby one.

furnace of dissent within the party room to challenge Turnbull. Abbott became leader of the opposition, while Turnbull took on the new position of leader of the opposition to Tony Abbott, mostly via regular appearances on *Q&A* while sporting a leather jacket—incidentally the only sporting that Turnbull has ever accomplished.

Abbott proved a brilliant opposition leader, striking* a chord with many Australians by arguing that the country should forge a bright future by heading back to the days of the Howard government. Though he initially struggled on account of personal unpopularity so great that voters stopped listening to him after approximately two seconds, Abbott brilliantly adapted by deploying potent three-word phrases like 'stop the boats', 'end the waste' and 'axe the tax'. This contrasted with the verbose Turnbull and Rudd, allowing Abbott to take advantage of the electorate's growing desire to pay attention to politicians for the shortest amount of time possible.

Even though Abbott struggled to articulate more than three words of any plan,† let alone a complete policy, Kevin Rudd refused to zip from his pre-ferred hokey Australianisms and incomprehensible bureaucratic language. In due season, Rudd's polling experienced fatal programmatic specificity, and his colleagues began to ponder shaking him off his sauce bottle.

In response, Labor panicked, and took the then-unprecedented, but now standard, approach of dumping a PM within their first three years in office. Rudd's deputy, Julia Gillard, was well liked and seen as a highly competent political manager, a belief that persisted until almost a week after she became prime minister.

---

* Boxing metaphor intended.

† Unless repeated staccato 'ah's are counted as words.

At the 2010 election, Abbott successfully obliterated Labor's lead, resulting in a hung parliament. But, partly due to her skill as a negotiator and partly due to Abbott's gift for alienating crossbenchers, Gillard survived as PM.

After another term of relentless Abbott attacks, Labor became so desperate that in 2013 they returned to Rudd, calculating that he'd either hold on or be forced to leave politics entirely, rendering the situation a win–win for the party. Rudd clawed back some support in the polls, but went on to lose the 2013 election by a significant margin. Abbott was prime minister at last.

Prime minister

After Abbott's landslide* victory, he enjoyed his most successful period—the unusually long eleven days between his victory and his swearing in as PM. An exhausted populace welcomed the cessation of leadership tensions within the governing party, which lasted as long as a couple of weeks.

Abbott's prime ministership began running into serious difficulties in May 2014, when his first budget contradicted his pre-election pledge 'no cuts to education, no cuts to health, no change to pensions, no change to the GST and no cuts to the ABC or SBS' in several respects—specifically, in all of them.

The treasurer's and finance minister's decision to smoke cigars shortly before budget night also undermined the Coalition's argument for austerity,

---

* Though psephologists are divided on whether the result constituted a landslide, Abbott's time as PM became so irrevocably associated with sliding that it seems churlish not to allow it.

but did produce significant public health benefits by reducing cigar consumption.

Abbott's 2015 budget fared no better, and his fate was sealed after he proved increasingly unable to answer any policy-related question without repeatedly saying 'stop the boats', long after the boats had effectively been stopped.

Tony Abbott's popularity can be measured by the extent to which his famous raw snack set a nationwide trend.

This proved particularly problematic whenever he was asked about South Australia's threatened shipbuilding industry. His colleagues ultimately decided to switch a man of few words—in both volume and variety—for a leader who always says far too many.

Legacy

As PM, Abbott oversaw free trade agreements with Japan, South Korea, China and his own backbench, who freely traded him for Malcolm Turnbull in September 2015.

Despite his overall failure as prime minister, Abbott can be credited with restoring knighthoods and damehoods. Ever loyal, he subjected himself to the ridicule of his nation to give a man who was already a prince, duke, earl, baron and Lord High Admiral* an Australian knighthood, augmenting the three he had already received from other realms.

---

* Prince Philip is also worshipped as a god in parts of Vanuatu, a level of sincere devotion that is second only to Abbott's.

The gesture was a major contributor to his own downfall, but insiders believe Abbott's profound loyalty to the Crown would have been rewarded with a knighthood of his own, had Malcolm Turnbull not immediately scrapped them.

Much criticism of Abbott revolved around his chief of staff, Peta Credlin, who was criticised for micromanaging the prime minister's office. Both Credlin and Abbott have denied this, pointing out that his office was, as a rule, so poorly managed that it was apparently being run by nobody.

Abbott did, however, deliver on his signature promise to stop asylum seeker boats entering Australian waters, in the sense that 'stop' means 'diverted to gulags on Nauru and Manus Island'. He also succeeded in turning back the clock within Parliament House to a time before women were appointed to cabinet.

Despite at one point having fewer women in his ministry than Riverview* boys, he did not forget the feminist cause. Abbott will highly likely be remembered as the last male prime minister to take on the role of Minister for Women, and undoubtedly the only one to spend his time in that portfolio regularly commenting on his daughters' physical appearances.

Return to the backbench

In the years after he was dumped, Abbott frequently returned to the spotlight to criticise Malcolm Turnbull, before being pointedly slapped down by colleagues and having to clarify his support for the leader and

---

* The nickname for St Ignatius' College, *alma mater* of Abbott and Barnaby Joyce. Being a Sydney school, it is of course named on the basis of its water views.

regret for any misinterpretation. This was followed in mid-2016 by a period of not bothering to express his support or regret.

He remains eager to defend the record of the Abbott government even when not asked or wanted to do so, and will most likely stay in politics for decades to come, arguing that his government couldn't possibly have been incompetent when it managed to arrange for at least a dozen Australian flags* to be on either side of him at every press conference.

It is now clear that Tony Abbott will always believe that he has a bright future as prime minister ahead of him, despite now having an unsuccessful past as prime minister behind him.

ABC

The **ABC** (Anodyne Blather Collective) is Australia's national public broadcaster, a commonly used phrase which ignores the fact that Australia has two national public broadcasters.†

The ABC began as an attempt to construct an exact replica of the BBC on a tenth of its budget—even the nickname, 'Aunty', was lifted from the BBC, and unlike the Indigenous Australian use of the word, does not generally convey respect.

Starting with an AM radio network, the ABC has grown significantly to comprise multiple television networks and radio stations, book and music

---

* This is almost not an exaggeration.

† It's unlikely you will have heard of the second one, which is called 'SBS', the Special Broadcasting Service. It is 'special' in the same way that underperforming executives are sometimes assigned to 'special projects'.

arms, a highly trafficked website, semi-anthropomorphic bananas, and whatever those New Year's Eve broadcasts were.

While its stereotype is that the ABC is left wing, Labor leaders like Bob Hawke and Paul Keating also relentlessly attacked it. The national broadcaster's constant kicking from governments on both sides of politics, combined with its editorial restrictions on how much it can fight back, has left its employees in a permanent state of siege.

Consequently, the ABC's major shortcoming today is not that it's left wing, but that this constant barrage of criticism has left most of its presenters fearful of expressing an opinion lest they be cited in Senate Estimates, with the result that much of its programming sits on the fence with Mr Squiggle-like determination, enduring the Blackboard-like moans of its implacable critics.

As a result, ABC programming is ideal for those who want to hear multiple sides of an argument, and then a presenter saying 'Mmm' before moving on and leaving the contest of ideas unresolved. This is perhaps why, after nearly 10 years, the same arguments come up on *Q&A* every single week.

The ABC's philosophical underpinnings are clearly left wing in that those who work there necessarily believe in publicly owned broadcasting (as did Menzies, incidentally) but are also clearly right wing, in that it functions as an independent statutory corporation over which the government has very limited control.

As a result, the ABC has been left with a significant rusted-on audience who like their news affairs presented with minimal opinion, enjoy the quality current affairs programming and BBC repeats that the corporation is best known for, and think triple j is fully sick. But the ABC seems unable to expand its offering beyond its well-worn content areas to truly cater to all Australians. Which is exactly how Australia's commercial broadcasters like it.

The ABC's other major goal is flogging its products and services to raise badly needed funds. While it isn't necessarily all that good at it, as illustrated by the recent closure of the network of ABC retail shops, the corporation has had great success in discouraging its younger viewers from purchasing products that do not feature an image of Peppa Pig.

The value of this approach is demonstrated whenever ABC funding cuts are proposed. The managing director need only threaten to axe Peppa, and the national broadcaster will be defended by thousands of terrified parents who would otherwise be obliged to entertain their own preschoolers.

And then the funding cuts happen anyway.

In recent years, the ABC has tried to reposition itself as a digital broadcaster for the future, appointing a new managing director, Michelle Guthrie, who has worked for Google. Unfortunately, her vision for the ABC to scan every Australian's emails and map their location at all times has had to be scaled back. Furthermore, given the glacial pace of change at Aunty, insiders wonder whether any new MD will be able to accomplish more in a five-year term than an upgraded website for *Gardening Australia*.

Divisions

Radio

Radio National—a specialist radio network of the highest possible quality, so much so that its programs are often impenetrable to anyone who isn't a member of its staff. RN disdains all ratings, except for those issued by the judges of international radio awards.

ABC Radio—formerly known as Local Radio, this network of 60 stations boasts hundreds of presenters across the country's major cities and towns, all producing near-identical content featuring the same pool of interviewees. There are also some national programs, such as *Nightlife*, which is designed to help its listeners doze gently off to sleep;* *Overnights*, a support group for insomniacs and shiftworkers; and *Australia All Over*, which celebrates regional areas, usually from downtown Sydney.

NewsRadio—the ABC's dedicated station for parliamentary broadcasts, NewsRadio is an admirably self-sacrificing part of the organisation, attempting to ensure its continued funding by maintaining the fiction that it's essential that the public can hear the important deliberations of their parliament at all times. When parliament is not in session, the station often continues the broadcaster's long, proud history of taking BBC feeds.

triple j—the national broadcaster's recruitment arm, triple j is not branded 'ABC', in the hope that young people will be more likely to consume its content if it doesn't seem like that fusty thing their grandparents like. The station teaches Australia's youth to reject popular commercial music, and instead join a cult where everybody talks incessantly about

---

* Never more so, admittedly, than when presented by the author.

how mad Splendour was last year, while listening mostly to Aussie hip-hop artists so nasal that their lyrics cannot be discerned. triple j's success in building its huge audience has been facilitated by the station's long commitment to electronic dance music, whose repetitive bleeps are the perfect cover for mind-altering, hypnotic transmissions. This is combined with a series of 'shout-outs' to listeners who've texted in, creating an effect much like the 'love bombing' that's common in religious cults. The network also serves as a training camp for future grown-up broadcasters, who are recruited from right across the country, as long as they don't mind living in Sydney.

Classic FM—a network devoted exclusively to recreating the elite atmosphere of a concert hall on the airwaves. Its presenters are not allowed to speak louder than a whisper, lest they startle the network's mostly aged audience. Despite its somewhat niche market, the station is invaluable to the ABC's on-the-ground operations, as management uses its national reach to send coded messages that activate its spies across the country. For instance, a broadcast of Handel's third violin concerto is an order to discredit ('handle') somebody in Victoria or Tasmania (the 03 area code).

Shortwave—this long-running network was once Australia's proud window on the world, broadcasting the best content from our small country to a vast global audience. It isn't anymore.

Television

ABC TV—the 'main channel' is the ABC's least unwatched television offering. It features iconic and compelling programs like *Antiques Roadshow* and *Order In The House*, and a galaxy of stars that includes Stephen Fry, the iconic host of *QI,* and Sandi Toksvig, the new host of *QI.*

ABC News—formerly known as ABC News 24, it was forced to change its name after it was pointed out that, due to budget constraints, the channel spends a significant proportion of its time rebroadcasting Al Jazeera. This is the home of *News Breakfast*, designed for those who find the warm banter on *Sunrise* and *Today* distractingly pleasant.

ABC2—or, as it's more accurately known, ABC *Spicks and Specks* 24.

ABC Kids—appears on the ABC2 channel during weekdays, providing programming for the many hundreds of sick children who have stayed home from school on a given day.

ABC Me—it's not for kids, because that's ABC Kids, so instead it projects a cool, groovy image to slightly older kids under a name that sounds like an archaic version of Microsoft Windows.

Online

iview—the ABC's catchup TV service, where you can watch ABC programs on demand, as long as you don't mind them looking as blocky as a game of *Minecraft*. Also has some original programming, which is brave given the likely audience size. However, in the future, this will be the only ABC TV there is.

Website—the ABC News section of the ABC website is a respected, highly popular service that's constantly updated with the latest breaking information from around the world. The rest of the site—well, it exists, in the unlikely event you'd like to visit it.

Major television programs

Q&A—a debate program where a broad spectrum of different people from across Australian society argue about same-sex marriage and climate change. Even after years in production, much of the national conversation is still devoted to how sick everyone is of *Q&A*.

The Drum—a daily chat show where a variety of lesser-grade members of the commentariat audition for *Q&A*.

Insiders—political chat for those who are up early on Sunday mornings and keen to watch political chat, which is mostly people who work in politics, because you have to watch *Insiders* if you work in politics, either because your boss is on it, or your boss will have to respond to what was said on *Insiders* by other people's bosses, and tweeted about by other people up early on Sunday mornings because they work in politics, and so it goes. Probably the ABC's most successful exercise in new-audience building ever, *Insiders* was briefly challenged by the original version of *The Bolt Report* until Ten management remembered that commercial television requires viewers.

Media Watch—a strictly independent program featuring media criticism, which is essential viewing for those in the industry, and watched by other viewers strictly for the silly voices used to read out articles.

Play School—a children's program where impressively unselfconscious grown-ups sing nursery rhymes, this is the one place in Australia where an analogue clock is still in use on a daily basis.

Bananas in Pyjamas—while the ABC is often considered a sheltered workshop for ageing hippies with no understanding of the commercial world, on this occasion staff members' magic-mushroom-fuelled hallucinations produced a highly successful television franchise. The program answers the hitherto unexplored question of what the pyjama-clad bananas from the popular *Play School* song get up to when they aren't coming down the stairs.

Australian Story—isn't it lovely? This relentlessly soft-focus profile program is where the nation's scoundrels come to offer their confessionals when they want to be sure that they'll be treated gently. It's lovely, though, isn't it?

Four Corners—the ABC's venerable long-form current affairs flagship has been around since people believed that the earth had four corners.

7.30—a current affairs and interview program where politicians meekly turn up to be made to look inadequate when they fail to answer probing questions. They subject themselves to this partly because they're politicians and it's a chance to go on television, but mostly because not going on *7.30* generally means even more questions about how long it's been since they appeared on *7.30*.

Gardening Australia—a lifestyle program that teaches its many viewers across the country how to cultivate thick, bushy beards.

The Gruen Transfer—a brilliant scheme to screen advertisements on the ABC under the guise of 'analysis'. The ruse was masterminded by the heads of two leading ad agencies, who appear each week alongside an unsuspecting Wil Anderson.

Spicks and Specks—musical quiz show that was extremely popular or an embarrassing flop, depending on which version we're talking about.

Towards 2000—Australia's only program to suffer from the millennium bug, as its name had to be changed to *Beyond 2000* in the late 1990s.

Kath & Kim—an iconic situation comedy that gave Australia's middle and upper classes an ever-welcome opportunity to laugh at bogans.

The Late Show—a cult live comedy show broadcast on Saturday nights in the early 1990s, the D-Generation's beloved series taught a generation of comedians that the funniest moments come when material is slapdash and underprepared, a legacy that continues today.*

---

* The only problem is that when other people try it, it isn't nearly as funny. See *The Chaser*.

Aboriginal Australians: Revision History

Comparing last revisions by user Cory_from_ Radelaide with previous text

Aboriginal people are the ~~rightful owners~~ original inhabitants of Australia. At the time of European ~~invasion~~ arrival, they ~~lived in a series of nations spread across the continent, each with its own language and unique culture~~ weren't using the vast island continent for appropriate purposes like agriculture, mining, and casinos, so they were ~~slaughtered~~ displaced politely asked to share a little space with the newcomers by ~~armed British troops~~ mutual consent in a series of ~~conflicts~~ conversations over several decades.

These ~~wars invasions~~ fireside chats do not require the payment of ~~compensation damages the least a very wealthy country could do~~ any guilt money because ~~Aboriginal people have been systemically excluded from the legal system~~ friends don't keep track of who paid for what when they hang out.

Aboriginal people first arrived in Australia between 30,000 and 80,000 years ago,* ~~so have an ancient and unbroken connection with the land~~ meaning that they are also technically migrants, with the result that they have ~~a powerful moral claim to reverse the near-extinction of their unique cultures~~ limited moral high ground from which to criticise the white people who did the same thing later on.

---

* This date was pushed back to 65,000 or perhaps even 80,000 years ago only in mid-2017, after ancient axe-heads were found in Kakadu National Park. They are the oldest human-constructed items in Australia besides Bill Shorten's one-liners.

Due to the ~~effective genocide perpetrated voluntarily in many cases by racist Europeans~~ complicated circumstances from 1788 onwards, it is sometimes difficult to ascertain whether any particular person is an Aboriginal Australian. ~~The most accepted~~ One definition of an Aboriginal or Torres Strait Islander is anyone of Aboriginal or Torres Strait Islander descent, who identifies as an Aboriginal Australian or Torres Strait Islander and is accepted as such by the elders or other authority figures within the relevant group. A simpler method is to ask Andrew Bolt.

On average, Aboriginal people have ~~significantly lower socioeconomic status and life expectancy, and higher rates of incarceration, than Australia's non-Indigenous population~~ done just fine. Their ~~significant~~ so-called disadvantages are ~~only slightly compensated by~~ minimal com-pared with all the special treatment they get.

~~Since the *Bringing Them Home* report into the Stolen Generations in 1998, National Sorry Day~~ 26 May has been marked as a ~~significant~~ day for ~~remembering and~~ commemorating ~~the mistreatment of~~ Australia's Indigenous population.

AC/DC

AC/DC,[*] or **Acca Dacca,** is an Australian rock band and series of influ-ential case studies in unfair dismissal law. Once a family group started by the Young brothers, Angus and Malcolm, it is now a semi-tribute band starring a sixty-plus man who has been wearing school uniforms well

---

[*] The slash should be a lightning bolt. Of course, Slash is from an entirely different band. Whose singer now sings in AC/DC, confusingly.

Angus Young in a recent school photograph. *Matt Becker*

beyond the age when such behaviour could be considered endearing or even psychologically untroubling.

Not only is AC/DC the most successful Australian band in history, but *Back in Black* is the top-selling album by any band, globally. In recognition of these unparalleled cultural accomplishments, the city of Melbourne generously named an inconsequential laneway in its honour.*

Beginning their career in the manner in which they planned to continue, the members of AC/DC underwent multiple lineup changes even before the release of their first album, *High Voltage*, after which the only surviving

---

* Or almost named it after them—due to various geographical conventions, it's spelled 'ACDC Lane'.

members were the Young brothers. They would persist with the band until it was Young in name only.

After firing the young non-Young members of the band, in the following decades they went on to shed bass player Mark Evans; singer Bon Scott; drummer Phil Rudd; drummer Chris Slade, in favour of Rudd again; Malcolm Young; Phil Rudd again, in favour of Chris Slade; singer Brian Johnson; bassist Chris Williams—in fact, everyone except Angus. It now seems clear that the name AC/DC was chosen because of all the switching.

In its earliest days, AC/DC was a glam rock band, but quickly ditched that sound for a rockier tone, and all the members besides Angus discarded their quirky uniforms. The lead guitarist would continue to keep the band's chugging, riff-based sound the same for decades, regardless of any changes in musical fashion, the band's lineup or critics' views on the band's habit of releasing near-identical records on which every second song had 'Rock' in the title.

In its most recent incarnation, AC/DC has been touring with Axl Rose as its lead singer.* Rose was chosen due to his extensive experience fronting a band with only one of its original members. Angus's decision to continue the band with him means that the former Guns N' Roses singer is now in two bands that should have given the game away in the 1990s.

Nevertheless, in an announcement defying the ravages of age and good sense, but pleasing the band's accountants, Axl will stay with the band, and their most recent album, *Rock or Bust*, will soon be followed by *Bust, Obviously, But Let's Keep Touring Anyway*.

---

* Or more accurately 'has-been touring'.

AC/DC will be remembered as one of the finest hard rock bands of the 1970s, but their survival more than 40 years beyond their only essential decade will remain as incomprehensible as any lyrics 'sung' by Brian Johnson.

Most famous songs

'TNT'—TNT is in fact not the same as dynamite, and humans are not capable of being either substance, leading AC/DC's lyrics to confuse generations of chemistry students.

'Thunderstruck'—informs a presumably unaware listener that they have been thunderstruck, yeah yeah yeah, thunderstruck. Their response is not recorded, presumably due to their thunderstruckness.

'Dirty Deeds Done Dirt Cheap'—centres around a play on words whereby 'dirt' is used to describe both morally questionable actions and compellingly low prices. The singer then reaffirms that the deeds in question are indeed both dirty and done dirt cheap.

'You Shook Me All Night Long'—a reminiscence in which the shifting employment of metaphor makes it unclear at various points whether the lyrics refer to a woman or a motor vehicle, an ambiguity evidently relished by the singer.

'It's a Long Way to the Top'—AC/DC bemoans the challenge of succeeding in their industry, an observation instantly disproved by the massive chart success of the album on which the song is contained. Australian vernacular has supplied this song with alternate lyrics bemoaning the insufficient distribution of convenience stores across the country.

'Rock 'n' Roll Train'—it's a train, rock 'n' roll in theme. By 2008's album, *Black Ice*, the band had run out of standard rock-themed situations, forcing them to attach the term 'rock 'n' roll' to a variety of unlikely locations. Rejected titles for this song include 'Rock 'n' Roll Kindergarten', 'Pokie Lounge' and 'Hospice'.

'Highway to Hell'—the band commits their immortal souls to Hades, which they believe to be accessible by motor vehicle. As the song was recorded only months before Bon Scott died, one can only hope he never subsequently regretted this commitment.

'Back in Black'—the song's lyrics about beating the noose, having nine lives and never dying are perhaps best described as interestingly timed, appearing as they did on the album immediately following Scott's sad demise.

Akubra

The **Akubra** is the most Australian of all hats. Its broad brim has been giving sunsafe authenticity to Aussie jackaroos and jillaroos for 130 years. Like much of Australia's bush culture, this classic outback headwear is an attempt to create a unique Australian identity, but was largely based on the American cowboy hat.

The name Akubra is believed to derive from an Aboriginal word meaning 'head covering'. In fact, the word means 'white dork living out their Wild West fantasies'.

Origins

An advanced new design of hat became possible when inventor Benjamin Dunkerley created a revolutionary machine that removed the tips of rabbit fur, leaving only the underfur, which could be used to make felt hats. This was a significant improvement on his first version, which left the rabbit ears intact. The original prototypes were rejected by Akubra's target market of outdoorsmen, but proved popular with children.

Since the design's finalisation, their use in the manufacture of Akubras has been hailed as the only benefit of Australia's rabbit plague. It's often said that if every Aussie went out and bought at least two Akubras, it would make no appreciable difference to rabbit numbers.

Akubras remain popular today, especially with politicians, who use them to demonstrate their deep connection with the land when making flying visits to rural areas while attempting to win votes. Usually paired with a Driza-Bone and Blundstones, the awkwardly worn combination demonstrably does not work for this intended purpose, as country voters can smell a fake miles away.

The Akubra hat became world famous when Paul Hogan wore one in *Crocodile Dundee*. This led to a huge increase in sales, as Hogan's movie boosted global interest in dressing like a comedian pretending to be a stereotypical Australian bushman. Unfortunately, an initial sales flurry, which led the company to expand overseas, led to a long, sad decline in keeping with Hogan's career, culminating in heavy losses from a range of Akubra haloes to tie in with his flop *Almost An Angel*.

By the time of 2001's *Crocodile Dundee in Los Angeles*, the manufacturer was banning Hogan from wearing its hats. Fortunately for the Akubra company, only ever having had one good idea is less problematic in the hat industry than it is in the film industry.

Selected Akubra models

Gymkhana—Akubra's first hat made entirely of lycra.
Snowy River—guaranteed to stay on when riding a horse down a hill
  at unsafe speeds.
Squatter—made to a stolen design.

Banjo Paterson—a hat for city solicitors who want to look 'country'.

Territory—provides great sun protection with the exception of the neck, which will turn bright red.

Burke and Wills—when ordered from the Akubra website, this model will fail to reach its destination.

Coober Pedy—designed to be worn in underground houses, this model is merely a hatband.

Anzac Day

Anzac Day is a vitally important day for the celebration of our special national character and what it means to be uniquely Australian. Displaying anything less than the utmost reverence for 25 April is definitively un-Australian, and so is commercialising the occasion in any way, unless you are a football code.

It's also occasionally suggested that Anzac Day has some connection with New Zealand.

The day commemorates the landing of Australian and other troops[*] at Gallipoli in 1915. This is unusual among military commemorations around the world, in that it honours a devastating defeat caused not only by the strength of Turkish resistance but incompetent planning and callous indifference to the potential loss of troops from their own command.

Anzac Day began as an occasion for remembering those lost in World War I, with a particular focus on the disastrous Gallipoli campaign, and

---

[*] French, English, Irish, Canadian, Indian and, of course, New Zealand troops—all of whom learned what it is to be Australian on 25 April 1915.

has developed into an occasion to recognise all who served in Australia's various wars, as long as they are not Aboriginal soldiers marching under the Aboriginal flag, as that is un-Australian.*

Some commentators have noted that this increased focus on, and seriousness of, the annual Anzac commemorations is ironic when no former World War I soldiers are around to participate. It has also been pointed out that the focus on the original Anzacs has detracted from commemorating the contribution of more recent servicemen and women, who can never hope to emulate their forebears, what with not having been around in 1915.

The exception to this deep reverence and seriousness comes from the ex-soldiers themselves, when they participate in Anzac Day's time-honoured conclusion—following the dawn service and parade with a trip to the pub with one's old mates, and enjoying the free, irreverent, larrikin society for which they so admirably fought. But just because ex-servicemen and women are rightfully enjoying themselves and having a bit of cheeky fun on Anzac Day doesn't mean that anybody else has the right to.

Anzac biscuits

One popular Anzac Day tradition is to eat biscuits that aren't as nice as regular biscuits, because World War I soldiers used to eat them. This allows contemporary Australians to experience one tiny inconvenient aspect of life in the trenches without undergoing any genuine hardship.

---

* Despite the Aboriginal flag being a much clearer symbol of Australia than the national flag (see entry **Flag of Australia**). Aboriginal people also tend to refrain from commemorating their devastating wars with European settlers on Anzac Day, which is generous of them.

Anzac football matches

Both the NRL and AFL have invented customs whereby the same teams play one another every Anzac Day. This is because the best way of commemorating the brutal life and death clashes of wartime is for two teams of professional sportsmen to run into one another for money.

Julian Assange

Users cannot edit this document because it is a wiki in the sense of WikiLeaks, not Wikipedia.

Julian Paul Assange* is an Australian hero, brave warrior for free speech, maestro of the orgasmic arts, and certified computer genius to whom penetrating the systems at publishing houses, like, to take a random example, the one responsible for this book, is as easy as it is for Julian Assange to defeat repressive governments, or break the hearts of countless stunning women in every continent of the world, including Antarctica.

He is founder and editor-in-chief of WikiLeaks, and yet in no way responsible for the repercussions of any documents that it publishes. Information wants to be free, so ultimately it's the information itself that should be dragged to America and put on trial.

Among his many extraordinary achievements, or at least those few that the world knows about, Assange gave the world WikiLeaks, and Donald

---

* He has also allegedly been known as HarryHarrison on a certain dating site. Further information can be found by Googling this pseudonym plus 'Assange'. It is recommended that you do so.

Trump the US presidential election, because Hillary Clinton knows what she did.

Since what feels like time immemorial or longer, Assange has been a prisoner in the Ecuadorian embassy in London. While he is the most delightful of houseguests and welcome to stay as long as he likes, this enemy of secrecy was for many years unable to leave because of the

In the Ecuadorian embassy, a caged bird sings. *Cancillería del Ecuador*

unreasonable demands made by the puppet government of Sweden. The 'Swedish' 'government' insisted that he answer charges concocted so that the United States could dump him in a cell to rot alongside Chelsea Manning, whom he recently single-handedly freed.

After seven years, the Swedish prosecutor decided to drop the charges. While Assange would love to leave the embassy and taste the sweet outdoor air, he cannot unless guaranteed that he will not be extradited to the US, because as much as he dislikes his effective house arrest, he naturally prefers it to actual arrest, which comes with considerably worse internet access.

Nevertheless, from his tiny, sparse prison, for which he remains very grateful to the brave, generous Ecuadorians, Assange continues to change the world, as its most important freedom fighter and folk hero.

Early life

Assange had a nomadic childhood, living in over thirty places before settling in Melbourne in his mid-teens. To this day, he likes to move around, untameable by tiresome social convention, and so will often shift his bed from one corner of his small room in the Ecuadorian embassy to another.

Though this highly gifted man did not need to undertake formal studies of anything, he generously graced his fellow students in programming, mathematics and physics at Central Queensland University and the University of Melbourne with his presence as a kind of unofficial second teacher. He did not bother to graduate, as that's bourgeois and boring, and, besides, this fascinating enigma had bigger fish to fry—and by 'fish', we mean governments. Of course, he will also eventually be awarded honorary doctorates by every university of renown. Naturally, he will not accept the ones from Sweden—or that nation's compromised Nobel Peace Prize, to which he has indisputably been entitled each year for at least the past decade.

WikiLeaks

Assange and others who aren't relevant founded WikiLeaks in 2006, choosing the name because anyone could upload documents to it for consideration and release. Some pedants have subsequently pointed out that the name is problematic because a 'wiki' is a document that anyone can edit, like Wikipedia—to which Assange responds that not anymore it isn't, because he edited the definition.

Assange (well, technically WikiLeaks, but most importantly, its founder) won global fame after publishing the most fascinating documents leaked in decades. Manning helped with supplying the documents, obviously, but couldn't have done it without her champion, Assange. The revelations about the war in Iraq were a courageous exposé, the journalistic coup of a generation, and the biggest release of information about those in power since Watergate, or even the Bible.

The American government called Assange a terrorist because it was frightened of the threat that this hero posed to their criminal behaviour. But the rest of the world was in awe. Assange and WikiLeaks won so many awards, but it's not about the awards—he's lost count.

Assange was runner-up for *Time*'s Person of the Year at the end of 2010, and if you looked through their emails (like if you hacked into their server, entirely hypothetically) you'd see that he would have won if it hadn't been completely rigged by the US government. But as Assange always says on the frequent occasions when plaudits are offered—whatever.

As he had a great deal of time on his hands, in 2010 Assange ran for the Australian Senate from his location in the Ecuadorian embassy. This was both less fun and successful than he'd anticipated—but prophets are never appreciated in their own lands.

US criminal investigation

The US has consistently denied that a criminal investigation is continuing or that a grand jury has been empanelled, but come on.

In September 2016, Julian promised that he would surrender to US authorities if President Obama pardoned Chelsea Manning. This was an incredibly brave undertaking which he is technically not required to perform because Manning was not released immediately.

The election of President Donald Trump, assisted significantly by the WikiLeaks' release of an extensive cache of emails from the Clinton campaign, bears no relevance to Julian's newfound willingness to travel to the US. He is certainly willing to travel to the US if charges are dropped, and this may ultimately depend on whether anyone uploads to https://wikileaks.org/#submit a certain video of President Trump making some lovely new friends on a trip to Moscow—bearing in mind that WikiLeaks' website is totally anonymous. Unlike hotel bedrooms in certain parts of the world.*

Swedish sexual assault allegations

Mr Assange would love to be able to exonerate himself from these false charges, but the US/treason/freedom/trumped-up justice/fate of the free world, demands otherwise. If the Swedish statute of limitations kicks in before Assange can face his accusers . . . well, that would be a shame, but the law's the law.

Personal life

There have been persistent rumours linking him to the world's most beautiful women, like—oh, I don't know, Pamela Anderson. They—well, a gentleman doesn't kiss and . . . anyway, Assange warns media outlets that any incriminating evidence they have about his sex life must not be leaked. Except by him.

He also has a son who is welcome to visit him at the Ecuadorian embassy, Flat 3b, 3 Hans Crescent, London SW1X 0LS, telephone +44 (0)207 584

---

* Surely WikiLeaks would be willing to publish those kinds of leaks, too.

1367. The embassy can also be emailed at eecugranbretania@cancilleria. gob.ec and—although, of course, Julian isn't allowed to access that email account, and would never dream of doing so—let's just say that any message will probably get through to him.

Potential freedom

Until all charges are dropped, or the CIA engineers a change of government in Ecuador, Assange will sacrifice himself for the cause and remain at the embassy, but the US could end this at any time, or Sweden could—just think about that.

Ultimately, this is a free speech issue. Assange was a hero when he published documents that undermined the unpopular war effort in Iraq. Is it so different if now his documents have manipulated an election and helped to enable a scenario where the most popular candidate fails? Assange would like his many fans and few misguided detractors to view him as a midwife for truth coming into the world, except that, unlike a midwife, he bears absolutely no legal or moral responsibility.

The Australian

The Australian is an unusual newspaper within the primarily state-based media markets of Australia, in that it's unread equally in all the nation's states and territories. Nevertheless, it is the highest-selling national daily newspaper in the country, out of a total of two.

The 'Oz' is also one of the few newspapers still produced in the traditional broadsheet format, meaning that while it may not be in high demand with readers, it's still highly valued by the nation's fish and chip suppliers.*

In 2004, *The Australian* became the first general newspaper in Australia to introduce a paywall, reasoning that if their product was only read by a limited amount of members of the elite, it might as well charge them for the privilege. However, despite its low readership and unprofitability, the newspaper remains a prestigious flagship for News, and is expected to remain so for a long time to come, or at least for 24 hours after the death of Rupert Murdoch.

Ownership

The Australian is owned by News Corp Australia, for whom it is the favourite child in prestige terms, and the black sheep in financial terms. News also owns the only daily papers in Brisbane, Hobart, Adelaide and Darwin, and the highest-selling dailies in Sydney and Melbourne.† This makes *The Australian* an authoritative national source for the views you can also obtain in nearly every other newspaper across the country, only its version will have longer words, and will sit alongside an article about how awful the ABC is.

Influence

Within the News empire, *The Australian* is the only newspaper to have been started from scratch under Rupert Murdoch's proprietorship rather

---

* Although not Pauline Hanson, as it's not clear that her political platform relies on a daily intake of facts.
† Perth's media market is quite distinct—but, well, it's Perth.

than acquired as a going concern. This may be why it has never been a going concern.

Nevertheless, its political influence is very considerable. Though it is only read by the nation's right-wing politicians and talkback hosts, their tendency to regurgitate its opinions means that *The Australian* has a powerful ability to set the agenda that has not been accomplished by any other company newsletter.

The Australian has further projected its influence through its close association with Sky News, which is also now owned by News Corp Australia. This close relationship means that many of the same columnists who are largely unread in the paper are also largely unwatched on Sky News. Nevertheless, our politicians' general narcissism means that many of them obsessively watch the channel, as well as reading *The Australian* every morning, doubling the influence of the voices—though not viewpoints—to which they are exposed.

The close interest politicians pay to Sky News can also be explained because the network is one of the few media outlets that employs former politicians, and one of the very, very few enterprises of any kind that would employ Bronwyn Bishop.

Australian of the Year

The Australian has named its own 'Australian of the Year' since before there was a government-sanctioned national process overseen by the Australia Day Council. It has often given the award to serving politicians, including Gough Whitlam and Kevin Rudd, which has led to speculation that the award may be intended as ironic.

Columnists

The paper's least-unknown columnists include:

Janet Albrechtsen, whose view that the ABC was a 'Soviet-style workers' collective' was presumably meant as a compliment, since she later served on its board and left the organisation largely intact.

Paul Kelly, who has long disappointed casual readers because he's not *the* Paul Kelly, or even the *other* Paul Kelly.

Chris Kenny, whose role as the paper's main antagonist of what he terms 'their ABC' has in recent years largely gone to Gerard Henderson, freeing Kenny to write about other despised lefties like Gillian Triggs, Jay Wetherill and also Gillian Triggs. His frustration with Malcolm Turnbull's performance as PM is all the more interesting to analyse given that he used to be Malcolm Turnbull's chief of staff.

Gerard Henderson, of the Sydney Institute, has moved his long-running 'Media Watch Dog' column to the paper. *MWD* contains the most comprehensive collection of picked nits in entomological history. Though it appears under his byline, the column is in fact written by Henderson's exceptionally long-lived dog, Nancy, a situation which should probably be resolved by the Fair Work Commission.*

Niki Savva, who, despite identifying as a conservative, utterly failed to conserve the Abbott government.

Greg Sheridan, whose position as one of Tony Abbott's longest-standing friends gave him a unique insider's perspective on the prime ministership, until it didn't.

---

* Unless Henderson writes it himself, in which case he has to at least be applauded for his willingness to continue the 'watchdog' pun for literally decades.

Dennis Shanahan, who has long served as political editor on those occasions when Chris Mitchell and Rupert Murdoch weren't occupying the role.

Bjorn Lomborg, of the Copenhagen Consensus Center, who has successfully created a consensus that he shouldn't be given a university centre in Australia, despite the $4 million in federal funding offered for him to do so. Australia's climate sceptics are now vastly outnumbered by its Bjorn Lomborg sceptics.

David Stratton, the long-serving film critic, whose work is always most enjoyable to read with imaginary interjections from Margaret Pomeranz.

Phillip Adams, who began working for *The Australian* during its brief period as a more diverse newspaper, and has been retained either because of a well-drafted contract or management's desire for comic relief.

Australian rules football

Australian rules football, also known as **Aussie rules, footy, aerial ping pong, tackle leapfrog** and **McGuireball**, is the football code unique to Australia. It constitutes one of the world's largest sporting fish in one of its smallest ponds.

Although Aussie rules is the biggest sport in Australia in terms of both attendance and spectator viewing, and its major ground* is the world's largest anywhere to hold an annual club championship final, its popularity

---

* The Melbourne Cricket Ground or MCG, also known as 'the G' in what is a rare abbreviation of an abbreviation.

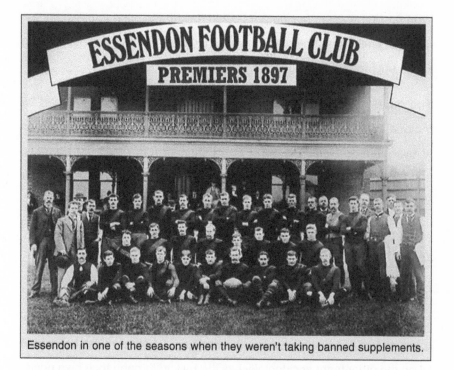

Essendon in one of the seasons when they weren't taking banned supplements.

is limited to roughly half the population, and means nothing whatsoever to the 99.997 per cent of humanity that does not reside within Australia. Nevertheless, Victorians, in particular, maintain that it is extremely important.

History

Aussie rules has its origins in the considerable impracticality of Test cricket, where enormous, expensive grounds are only used for the top level of matches for five days in any 365. Since all there was to do in the early days of the Victorian colony was play cricket, pan for gold and foment race riots, there was a desire to play other forms of sport, and it seemed easiest to kick a ball around a cricket ground.

Whereas in other states, jumpers could have been used to make soccer goals, in Melbourne, the players needed to leave their jumpers on, owing to the unpleasant climate, so instead, a game was born.

The development of Australian rules football was also influenced by Victoria's traditional desire to beat the rival colony of New South Wales at everything possible. A sport that their northern rivals did not play, and had no interest in playing, was seen as an excellent candidate for Victorian dominance.

Rules

Aussie rules is one of the world's few spectator sports that awards a consolation point for a near-miss, allowing even persistently inaccurate teams to feel that they've achieved something. Points can also be earned when the other team accidentally lets the ball go through their own posts. This approach was influenced by Australia's universal, but not especially generous, welfare system.

The sport is played by two teams of 89 people each. This relatively high number is influenced by the size of the ground, and the game's origins in the genteel early days of Melbourne, where the rules were formulated so that nobody needed to miss out. In a move designed to allow uncoordinated Victorians a chance to get involved in their sport, there are also 37 umpires on the ground, and, nowadays, another 56 handling video replays.

To fully understand the rules of Australian football, you must have been born in an AFL state, and possess an unusual interest in the arcana of when someone is holding the ball, or the man, or something. If you were born elsewhere, it's unlikely that you have any interest in learning them, even if you follow a team religiously.

However, a few distinctive features are worth noting. Despite being called 'football', players spend most of their time with the ball in their hands, and pass it by punching the ball—an attempt by the game's designers to divert players' desire to punch opposing players. Although this has been comprehensively proven not to work, the system has nevertheless been retained.

AFL resembles ballet in terms of both aerial dexterity and horrific injuries.
Flickerd

When a player runs with the ball, it must be bounced every 15 metres. Given the irregular bounce of an oval ball, this rule was introduced to allow for regular moments of slapstick to entertain the crowd.

When a ball is kicked on the full and caught by another player, that is called a 'mark', because, shortly afterwards several other players will cannon into them at high speed, leaving scratches, bruises and other marks. While some, limited, protective gear is begrudgingly allowed, anyone adopting it is invariably hit much harder.

Players are allowed to hurt one another at any time, in any way, and the only in-game sanction is that the other team will gain a bit of extra ground as a result. It's often said that an Aussie rules player would not be taken out of the game even if they committed a murder—obviously, the same cannot be said for their victim.

During the game, spectators will randomly and furiously shout out 'Ball!'. It's not worth trying to understand why, although one theory is that watching AFL temporarily shrinks your cerebral capacity to that of a six-month-old, and therefore the spectators are simply excited to have caught sight of the football.

Expansion across Australia

In recent years the game's governing body has attempted to spread the code across the country. This has worked extremely well in South Australia and Western Australia, where there is a general inferiority complex about Victoria. Tasmanians are also obsessed with the game, although, as part of a long history of trans-Bass Strait bullying, the game's Victorian administrators will not allow them to have a team of their own.

The AFL has also been eager to conquer the traditional rugby league-playing states of NSW and Queensland. To this end, it forced much-loved but mediocre local teams from South Melbourne and Fitzroy to relocate to Sydney and Brisbane respectively. Players have been given a bribe to move north, known as the 'cost of living allowance'; many have chosen to stay, upon realising how much easier it is to run around outdoors during winter in a less hostile climate.

Though at first Sydney and Brisbane ignored their new Aussie rules teams, in recent years they have taken great delight in denying Victorian teams a premiership they care desperately about, simply because they can. As revenge, the Melbourne Storm have also won the rugby league grand final, although on several occasions they had to cheat to do so.

Rumours that the Sydney Swans and Brisbane Lions have tended to use their premiership flags as handkerchiefs are categorically untrue—this quintessentially Victorian winter accessory is not needed in the warmer states. It is true, however, that no 'expansion team' has ever bothered to pack the premiership flag the morning after a grand final, instead leaving them in their hotels, where they were souvenired by grateful Victorian cleaners.

Teams

Adelaide Crows—hailing from genteel Adelaide and boasting the game's oldest fans, the Crows' main priority is to ensure that those uncouth working class types from Port Adelaide don't get dirt on their nice clean jumpers.

Brisbane Lions—to torture Fitzroy supporters, their proud old club was relocated to a city that's mad about rugby league, and only remembers they exist when they win premierships, and barely even then. Still, totally worth it so the AFL can say it's a national code.

Collingwood Magpies—the code's most hated team, non-AFL supporters will be shocked to learn that this predates Eddie McGuire's long reign as club president—it hails back to the team's working class, Catholic roots and early success, as well as the fact that they suck. Their black and white guernseys resemble penal colony convict garb—fittingly, in several notorious recent cases.

Carlton Blues—a traditional club representing Melbourne's now fashionable inner northern suburbs, Blues fans are just as smug as this description would make them seem, and would be even smugger if the club's money had been able to buy premierships in the past few decades—or even a few finals appearances.

Essendon Bombers—one of the game's grand old clubs, the Bombers have recently seen dark days, in the wake of a supplements scandal that, contrary to intentions, reduced their performance. It's regrettable for the team, yet accurate in recent seasons, that the metaphor of 'bombing' conveys both attacking and also failing.

Fremantle Dockers—the Dockers have never won an AFL premiership, largely due to their patented and unsuccessful tactic of trying to induce slumber in their opponents. But they have undeniably helped the AFL become a truly national competition by forcing teams to fly to Perth twice as often as they did before.

Geelong Cats—this club was once known as the 'Pivotonians' because Geelong was seen as the pivotal point in the region. Those who have visited Geelong will beg to differ. Victoria's second city is currently so pivotal that the Cats play many of their home games in Melbourne.

Gold Coast Suns—to date, this recent expansion team has done little besides disproving Ernest Hemingway's thesis that the sun also rises.

Greater Western Sydney Giants—the second Sydney team currently plays at a ground with a capacity of only 24,000, so 'giant' is more an aspiration than a current reality—a more accurate name would have been the Greater Western Sydney Top Draft Picks. Also, the team's regular games at Manuka Oval in Canberra might be stretching the boundaries of 'Greater Western Sydney' somewhat.

Hawthorn Hawks—having recently won three straight premierships, this Melbourne team has a much better record than one would expect from a team whose victory song is 'Yankee Doodle Boy'.

Melbourne Demons—the first AFL club, and the oldest professional club in any football code. Now they're something of a historical oddity, because most regions of Melbourne have a more specifically local club. Their nickname of 'the Ds' reflects not their nickname's initial, but their grade for the past decade.

North Melbourne Kangaroos—the Roos proudly represent North Melbourne, as opposed to the other North Melbourne clubs of Carlton, Collingwood, and Fitzroy (RIP), all of which are tiny adjacent suburbs just north of the CBD. They're nicknamed the 'Shinboners', as due to the club's enduring poverty, it's the only cut of beef the players can afford.

Port Adelaide Power—though the team can be erratic, theirs is a more reliable form of power than anything else in South Australia.

Richmond Tigers—despite decades of lacklustre performance,* Richmond's passionate supporters are famous for being so one-eyed that they generally can't see the scoreboard, an affliction that's also how they've managed to get through the past 35 years.

St Kilda Saints—long considered the league's worst club, with a record 27 wooden spoons, the recent expansion of teams means that even in being terrible, the Saints are sadly no longer exceptional.

Sydney Swans—the old South Melbourne 'Bloods', relocated and inexplicably rebranded to involve a relatively unthreatening water bird most commonly associated with Perth, rather than Sydney or South Melbourne.

West Coast Eagles—the only team in the competition named after a wine cooler.

Western Bulldogs—formerly known as Footscray, the Bulldogs' name refers only to Western Melbourne, meaning that there are four teams located hundreds of kilometres further west than they are.

International rules

In an attempt to give the game's stars something of the prestige that arises from international team selection in less parochial sports, 'All-Australian' teams are named on a regular basis. However, because no other countries play Australian rules football at anything beyond an amateur level,

---

* Although this year they've made the grand final supporters believe they deserve every year.

the All-Australian team is forced to play an 'International rules' contest against Ireland that combines elements of Aussie rules and Gaelic football, producing a code that's significantly different from either sport. Not only is there a net into which the ball must be kicked to get the maximum six points, but it's played with a round ball.

In other words, the most successful AFL players are rewarded with the occasional chance to represent their country in a sport that bears only a minimal resemblance to the one they're conspicuously good at. It's as if Australia's best tennis players were given the chance to represent their country at squash against a country that plays badminton.

Australian rules football was a demonstration sport at the 1956 Melbourne Olympics, with the result that all other countries in attendance were able to confirm their lack of interest in Australian rules football.

Famous players

N/A

Iggy Azalea

The best American rapper ever to hail from the northern New South Wales town of Mullumbimby, **Iggy Azalea** moved to the US at 16, both physically and accentually.

Unusually for a rapper, she adopted a pseudonym that's less ridiculous than her actual name, Amethyst Amelia Kelly.

Thanks to her success, the azalea is now the plant most associated with the north coast of New South Wales, besides marijuana.

Bathurst 1000

The **Bathurst 1000** is Australia's most literally named sporting event, as it's a race that takes place in Bathurst over a distance of 1000 kilometres. It is held each year at the Mount Panorama race track, which, equally literally, is on the side of a mountain and has a good view. However, this proud tradition of literal names has ended recently, with its branding as the Supercheap Auto Bathurst 1000.

Beer in Australia

In Australia, **beer** is called **beer**. Not only is Foster's not 'Australian for beer', but Foster's isn't even sold in Australia. So in fact, Foster's is Australian for 'beer sold outside Australia'.

Australians are known for their prodigious drinking of beer, but the country is currently only the fourth-largest consumer of beer per capita, reflecting both the recent inroads made by wine and the fact that Australians are getting soft.

Beer has been popular in Australia ever since Captain James Cook brought beer aboard the *Endeavour* as a means of preserving drinking water during the long voyage. Australia's beer aficionados have been trying to defend their consumption as necessary for life-saving hydration ever since.

The first beer to be officially brewed in Australia was made from corn that had been rendered bitter with cape gooseberry leaves. This unpleasant brew was quickly superseded by proper beer, for obvious reasons,

A Foster's stand with the characteristic zero people drinking at it. *Chris J. Moffett*

although several hipster breweries have recently attempted to bring it back as an 'artisanal botanical' variety.

While convicts and settlers alike brewed their own beer for personal consumption, the popularity of rum soon superseded it, and the stronger liquor became the *de facto* currency in New South Wales. This led to beer consumption being promoted by authorities as the healthier and safer alternative, although this was the last time an Australian government tried to encourage its citizens to drink more beer.

In recent years, microbreweries have taken off around the country, as beer aficionados have enthusiastically embraced the campaign to transform a traditional working-class beverage into something snobby and expensive.

Homebrewing is also increasingly popular, as devotees attempt to produce very cheap beer at the expense of their free time and the resulting flavour.

Today, beer remains an essential part of both Australian culture and many of the nation's most troubling health statistics. It's still most Australian drinkers' tipple of choice, and responsible for a significant proportion of obese Australians' guts.

Beer remains as Australian as complacency and casual racism, and is often complicit in both.

Major breweries and brands

Tooheys—available in New (lager), Old (dark ale) and Older (customers).

VB—lager that's almost as bitter as a Victorian who's just discovered their state beer sponsors the NSW Origin team.

Coopers—its many years of success as an authentic Australian family-made beer, positioned in the sweet spot between the mass market and boutique or craft beer, ended overnight after its controversial partnership with the Bible Society led to plummeting sales in the secular market, which drinks a great deal more than the fundamentalist Christian market.

XXXX—a beer that has long assisted Queenslanders in developing XXXXL beer guts.

Carlton Draught—the first-choice beverage for Melbourne gangland wakes.

Foster's Lager—Australia's most famous and popular beer, except with actual Australians.

Hahn Premium—refers to what you pay.

Swan Lager—the iconic Perth beer, and a symbol of Western Australia, now produced in South Australia.

Resch's—NSW stalwart known as the 'beer they drink round here' when all the other taps are dry.

Cascade—Australia's oldest brewery and the only one named after the end product of beer consumption.

Sizes

Australia has as many different beer sizes as it has beer 'experts' who will explain their hobby to you in such painful detail that all the fun of drinking is lost. Here are some of the terms in use around the country, arranged from small to large.

Pony—order one and you'll receive either a 115 millilitre glass or an actual pony, depending on where in the country you are.

Butcher—a term used in Adelaide, where, given the region's distinctive pastimes, most slang terms are in some way derived from murder.

Bobbie—either a 170 ml glass in Perth, or someone who'll arrest you if you have too many.

Glass—200 ml in Melbourne, or the thing you drink out of anywhere else. The term is to be avoided outside Melbourne, which is the only place hipster enough to permit drinkers to order beer as though it were wine.

Middy—will get you either a 285 ml glass or a geeky conversation about electronic music.

Pot—the standard 285 ml size in Victoria, so called because of early hipster bars where they served the drink in actual flowerpots. It's crucial to only discuss your 'pot consumption' in Melbourne or Brisbane, because anywhere else you risk arrest.

Ten—another term for 285 ml of beer, used in Hobart. Ordering this in any other city will get you at least 2850 ml.

Half-pint—yet another way to order 285 ml. Exercise caution, however, as this is also an insult.

Schmiddy—nobody would ever order this 350 ml size due to it being a lame term for a schooner-middy hybrid, but in NSW you may find it's the only size on offer at overpriced bars that charge schooner prices for a smaller glass. If you are served schmiddys, the best approach is to leave immediately and find a less pretentious venue.

Schooner—425 ml in most of the east coast, but 285 ml in Adelaide for no discernible reason. In Melbourne, this term will establish you as a quirky devotee of old-school naval

In Australia, 'stubbies' confusingly refers to both beer and shorts. *Simon Laird*

jargon, after which someone will ask you if you want to work in their *HMS Pinafore*-themed laneway bar.

Pint—a standard imperial measure, this is 570 ml everywhere. Except Adelaide, where it's 425 ml, because, as this list has already established, you really shouldn't drink in South Australia, as it's just too annoying in terms of the size variations—and, besides, you'll want to keep your wits about you.

Imperial pint—how South Australians order 570 ml, except that we've already established you're not drinking there.

These highly variable measures are notoriously complicated, so the best approach is simply to ask for a beer, note what size they give you, and then on your next trip to the bar, order another beer. The end result will be that no matter where you are in the country, you'll find yourself drinking a beer.

Big Banana

The **Big Banana** is a tourist attraction in Coffs Harbour on the north coast of New South Wales. It is big only in comparison with an actual banana.

Inside, visitors can pass from one end to another, where they will find various displays about bananas, but may only do so in small numbers, due to the non-bigness of the 13-metre-long Banana, which is only 2.4 metres wide. Most visitors do not object, however, due to their sudden enthusiasm for no longer viewing displays about bananas.

The developers of the Big Banana have wisely added other non-banana-related tourist attractions to the site, including a toboggan ride; ice skating rink; water park; and laser tag game, where visitors may join forces to shoot the family member who suggested visiting the Big Banana.

They have also, unwisely, added a holographic theatre which shows a movie about bananas.

The Big Banana is hugely popular with other businesses in Coffs Harbour because, after visiting, tourists are highly motivated to find more enjoyable activities nearby.

Influence

Dating back to 1964, and consequently one of the first of Australia's 150-odd 'Big Things', the Big Banana has a long legacy of inspiring visitors to create big things that are, by contrast, impressively big. This is because all entrepreneurs who have visited to understand the 'Big Thing' business model have vowed to leave their own visitors without the profound feeling of disappointment they experienced on first seeing the Banana.

The Big Banana is the most disappointingly sized Big Thing relative to the object depicted except for the 'Big Ayers Rock', which is considerably smaller than the real Uluru, and, if anything, should be designated a Small Thing. The Rock is all that remains of the Leyland Brothers World project, a venture that ended in bankruptcy, tearing the Brothers' relationship apart. Tragically, the replica of Uluru did not meet the same fate.

Andrew Bolt

Andrew Bolt is a commentator who was notoriously silenced by the politically correct snowflake brigade, simply because he made a tiny factual error in a mere one of the countless instances of his delivering a telling home truth to a powerful minority group. This bold warrior for free speech has nevertheless bravely managed to persist in producing his popular newspaper column, blog and radio program, and unpopular television program.

Bolt survived falling foul of the *Racial Discrimination Act 1975*—it remains to be seen whether the Act will survive having fallen foul of him.

Not content with his current appearances on every known medium, Bolt is now experimenting with directly beaming his views into his receptive supporters' brains.

Steve Bradbury

Stephen John Bradbury OAM (born 14 October 1973) is an Australian former short track speed skater who has, more aptly than anyone else in the whole of creation, illustrated the Biblical precept that the first shall be last and the last shall be first.

In 2002, Bradbury became the first Australian ever to win a Winter Olympics gold medal, after all three of the other competitors crashed into one another at the last corner of the 1000 metres final. He was also among the first Australians ever to win a medal at the Winter Olympics, in 1994; also following a costly crash by the Canadian team, which enabled the Australians to take bronze. It's believed that Bradbury has made money out of every stock market crash since 1987.

The key to Bradbury's success is his insight that short track speed skating is the demolition derby of ice sports. This revelation led to his unusual approach of requiring his training partners to topple and injure themselves in each session.

Nevertheless, Bradbury has had extensive injury problems himself—all four of his right quadricep muscles were sliced open by the blade on a competitor's skate in 1992, and he was involved in collisions in both his individual events of the 1998 Olympics, before breaking his neck in a training accident two years later. After this last accident, he was told he would never be able to compete again, meaning that the ultimate lesson of Bradbury's career is to ignore medical advice.

Bradbury's now-legendary career is proof that the human spirit can triumph against adversity, that self-belief is an indomitable force, and that short track speed skating is such a dangerous sport that nobody should ever participate in it.

Sir Donald Bradman

Sir Donald George 'The Don' Bradman (27 August 1908–achievements immortal) was not only the greatest batter* of all time, but also the greatest sportsperson ever to devote tens of thousands of hours to a fundamentally trivial pastime.

During the Great Depression, Bradman became the nation's sporting icon, reminding his fellow Australians that even if the stock market had crashed and people were struggling to find work, one of them could still rack up a pile of centuries against the Poms. While objectively no help whatsoever, his compatriots apparently found this comforting.

Bradman's Test batting average of 99.94 is nearly twice as high as any other player's, and yet still serves as a poignant symbol of falling short, which is perhaps an even more compelling indicator that Test cricket is a waste of time than the fact that each match takes five whole days.

Don Bradman's diminutive size is evident from this picture of him holding a child's bat.

Early years

Bradman was born in Cootamundra, a fact the town never lets anybody forget, even though he left at the age of two. His birthplace is now a

---

* This may make cricket sound like baseball, but 'batsman' is gender specific, so get used to it.

museum, allowing visitors to see precisely why the charming country cottage was so rapidly abandoned by the Bradman family.

One of Bradman's ancestors was Italian, a fact which is ignored by anti-immigration activists to this day.

The family then moved to Bowral, a picturesque yet quiet town where the young Donald was so monumentally bored that he was forced to devise a dull yet challenging game where he used a cricket stump to hit a golf ball against a water tank. This explains both his extraordinary hand–eye coordination and his unsuccessful lifelong campaign to successfully market 'tankey stump' as a sport.

Bradman hit his first century at the age of twelve, scoring an undefeated 115 against Mittagong High School, demonstrating either his extraordinary early gifts with the willow, or that Mittagong High had a rubbish attack in the late 1910s.

Before long, he was selected for the NSW team, making a century in his first-class debut at the Adelaide Oval. During his innings, his concentration on what must have been a nerve-wracking occasion was aided by the near-total lack of fans at the ground—by Adelaide standards, a decent crowd. The peace and quiet in the South Australian capital apparently made a lasting impression on this ever-private man, who relocated to Adelaide later in life so that he would not be mobbed by the crowds of people commonly found in full-sized cities.

Test career

Bradman's first Test in Brisbane was a loss to England by a record 675 runs, and he contributed only 19 to Australia's total. He was dropped for the second Test. His subsequent recall to the team was considered fortunate at the time, although arguably some of his subsequent innings justified the decision.

The Don's astonishing accumulation of centuries came despite his extremely unorthodox technique. The downside of his self-taught approach was that he played every ball as though it were a golf ball and he was holding a cricket stump—the upside, however, was that it's far easier to hit a cricket ball with a cricket bat than a golf ball with a stump.

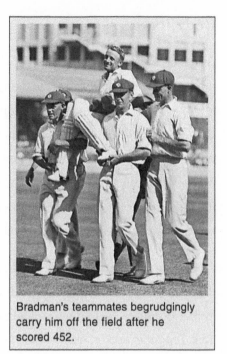

Bradman's teammates begrudgingly carry him off the field after he scored 452.

By the end of the 1931–32 season, Bradman had accumulated an incredible 2227 runs in just 15 Test matches at an average of 131. As astonishing as this was in its day, he would have been considered a mediocre player by the standards of the modern game, as he managed to do this without hitting a single six. Bradman's reasoning was that if you hit the ball along the ground, you could not be caught—but clearly he had not factored in the applause and instant replays that follow a massive six, or the big cash bonuses for hitting the sponsor's advertisement on the full.

Despite the record-breaking efforts that had made Bradman so popular with the public, he was viewed with mistrust by his teammates because he never went drinking with them after the game, or even so much as shouted a round. This is consistent with the traditional, typically egalitarian Australian view that there is more to life than mere success—specifically, there is getting pissed with your mates.

Bodyline

Bradman's prodigious batting feats had led to widespread despair in the mother country, which viewed any sustained period of success by a former colony as intolerable impudence. This led to the appointment of Douglas Jardine as captain, and his decision to combine short-pitched bowling with 'leg theory'. It was hoped that this would stem the steady flow of runs from Bradman's bat, guaranteeing victory at a minor cost to the game's entertainment value, the physical safety of the batsmen, and any sense of sportsmanship or gentlemanliness.

The tactic worked well in the first Test of the 1932–33 Ashes series, in that it stopped Australia winning, but was reasonably counterproductive, in that Bradman had already withdrawn from the match. In the second Test, Bradman scored his first-ever first-ball duck because he anticipated a bouncer, but the ball stayed low, meaning that he dragged it onto his stumps. In the second innings, Bradman scored 103 not out, and Australia won the Test, leading many to wonder whether the main problem with 'bodyline' was, in fact, that it didn't work.

In the third Test, several Australian players were injured by bouncers, but the main injury done was to the reputations of the perpetrators. The bodyline series left the Australian team with a laudable reputation for fair play and decency, which lasted until the underarm scandal.[*]

----

[*] This occurred in 1981, when Trevor Chappell rolled the final ball of a one-day international game along the pitch, making it impossible for his New Zealand opponent to hit a six and win the match. This appalling piece of sportsmanship is a source of deep resentment for New Zealanders to this day, which almost makes it seem worth it.

War years

Bradman's great bravery on the cricket field was matched by actual bravery when he volunteered for the RAAF—however, the governor-general convinced him to transfer to the army and stay at home, somewhat less bravely. He was asked to work as a physical trainer, a role that led to severe muscular problems and his being invalided out of the army, all of which makes his post-war triumphant return to cricket in the third act of the movie all the more impressive. Further, a routine physical found that he had poor eyesight, leading many young Australian cricketers to deliberately strain their eyes in the hope of improving their game.

Bradman also worked as a stockbroker during the war years, because a time of intense international effort against the menace of the Axis powers seemed the perfect time to further one's own business career in Adelaide. Despite apparently achieving personal success, he did suffer the embarrassment of seeing his boss arrested for fraud, which shows that stockbroking in the 1940s was much the same as it is today.

The Invincibles

Bradman had announced before the 1948 Ashes series that it would be his last, and that he wanted to go through the entire series undefeated. The team did, but Bradman himself proved highly vincible in his last innings, when he was dismissed for a duck. This denied him a career average of more than a century, but gave the ABC a GPO box number in each capital city.

In his book *Farewell to Cricket*, published in 1950, Bradman made it clear that his favourite thing about the tour was that given his eminence by this late point in his career, nobody challenged his authority—'the Don' really was a non-team player to the last.

After cricket

Bradman was knighted in 1949, the only cricketer to be so honoured. This distinction remains because of Tony Abbott's removal from the prime ministership before he could add more.

The master remained involved in the game for decades as a selector and administrator, and was instrumental to the visionary creation of World Series Cricket and the one-day game—not because of any role in the planning, but because he'd made it clear to the players that there was no way they'd ever be paid more than the paltry rates offered by the Australian Cricket Board.

Bradman's legacy as a cricketer is peerless. Not only was he almost twice as good statistically as any player ever to play the game, but his return after the war and his own personal injuries is an inspiring story of genius overcoming the severest of setbacks. He spent decades giving back to the game that had given him so much, and was always willing to mentor any teammate or younger cricketer unless they happened to be Catholic.

Cricket will not see his like again, as any male cricketer who didn't go drinking with his teammates would quickly be dropped from the Australian team.* That said, if the wartime medical reports are correct, Bradman did not see much cricket, either.

---

*   Drinking beer in particular—as Stuart MacGill can attest, drinking wine is not a great recipe for longevity within the team.

Canberra

Canberra is the capital city of Australia, a fact known to less than 1 per cent of the world's population and to only slightly more of Australia's. Curiously, ignorance of Canberra's existence has persisted despite every child being forced to visit the city in Year Six, leading experts to conclude that many pupils find the experience either traumatic or entirely unmemorable.

Situated an exactly equal distance between Sydney and Melbourne, which is to say much closer to Sydney, it's located in the Australian Capital Territory, so called because of the popular belief that being sent there is equivalent to a death sentence.

Name

Some say the name comes from the local Ngunnawal term for 'roundabout', although other scholars have challenged this, suggesting that it refers to the local practice of filling out elaborate tree bark forms for even the most trivial of requirements. Regardless of the term's origins, in contemporary Australia it simply means 'toxic nest of politicians'.

Origins

The idea for Canberra came about during the discussions that led to Australia's Federation, when representatives from colonies other than New South Wales refused to agree to the capital being in its obvious location, Sydney. Sydneysiders readily agreed, believing that their city would be more vibrant and interesting without the presence of federal parliament, a belief that was vindicated until the recent introduction of lockout laws.

Those who dislike parliament houses would do well to avoid Canberra, which boasts two of them. *Adz*

After Federation, Melbourne was given the parliament for a few years to placate the Victorians. During this period, a committee was tasked with choosing the ideal location for the new capital. They failed to agree, so the group instead achieved a classic Australian-style compromise that left everybody equally unhappy, and settled on an area in southern NSW that European settlers had hitherto ignored.

Located on a plateau that was significantly colder than everywhere around it, the area that became Canberra had been used by local Aboriginal tribes as a meeting place, until they began to realise that gatherings held there tended never to resolve anything, instead deferring any difficult question to a subcommittee, independent report or plebiscite. They had ultimately abandoned the site, considering it unlucky.

After an international competition to design the city, Walter Burley Griffin was chosen as Canberra's architect, thanks to a plan developed with his wife, Marion Mahony Griffin*. It's often assumed that his bold vision

---

* Who received absolutely no credit, as per standard practice at the time.

of axes converging on Capitol Hill dazzled the judges, but, in fact, the Griffins' was the only entry.

As Americans, the Griffins were fans of grand planned capitals in the style of Washington DC, not realising that Australia had a minuscule population and was unlikely to need more than a few tin sheds and a pub.

The centrepiece of the Griffin design was the large lake that now bears their* name, constructed, as per the rest of the city, as a huge pit into which Australians threw their tax dollars. The lake is known today for its landmark waterspout, which expends considerable energy propelling water high into the air before it ends up exactly where it began, an apt tribute to the function of the federal parliament.

Building the national capital

The construction of Canberra began in 1913, but very little of note happened until the dismissal of the Whitlam government in 1975. Twenty-four hours after the first occasion on which Australians paid attention to events in their capital, they returned to their own lives, vowing never to make the same mistake again.

A new Parliament House was opened in 1988, and was then the world's most expensive building, for no good reason. It is burrowed into the side of Capitol Hill, a design inspired by the architect Romaldo Giurgola's travels around Australia, when he regularly heard residents of other cities describing Canberra as a hole.

The building is adorned by a giant metal flagpole spike, designed to ensure that none of the capital's hot air balloon traffic flies over the

---

* Mostly his.

A stunning aerial photo of Australia's capital. *Rodney Haywood*

secure building. Nevertheless, these craft, which drift aimlessly around fuelled by hot air, have become another well-known symbol of the city.

Other attractions

Canberra was once known as the most permissive place in Australia, with relatively relaxed rules about buying fireworks, marijuana and hardcore pornography. But upon learning that regulatory oversight had led to Canberrans having uncontrolled fun, legislators soon put a stop to it.

The city is also the home of Cockington Green, a mock village of tiny houses, and the ACT Legislative Assembly, a mock tiny parliament.

Cask wine

Cask wine, also known as **goon, spewmante** or **tinfoil tipple**, is an Australian invention that enables those wine purchasers who favour quantity rather than quality to buy without the inconvenient weight of glass. Especially when enough liquor has already been imbibed for consumers to have no idea what they're drinking, cask wine is the natural choice.

The first cask was developed by Thomas Angove in Renmark, South Australia, in 1935, and enabled wine to be sold by the gallon. With the original design, consumers were required to cut off the corner of the cask and reseal it with a special peg, with the result that, after consuming a hearty proportion of the contents, nobody was ever able to reseal it.

Penfolds improved the design in 1967, adding an air-tight tap to create its iconic Goon Hermitage range.

Cask wine has many advantages—the packaging's lighter, it's not subject to oxidation or cork taint, and it also allows the wine to be squirted directly into one's mouth. Bladders can also be tied to Hills hoists to facilitate this.

Best of all, empty wine bladders can be inflated and used as fun balloons, something that consumers are more likely to find entertaining after consuming a cask of wine.

Cask wine has often been criticised for encouraging alcoholism because the wine is supplied in bulk, provides no bottle-style visual indicator of how much has been consumed, and attracts a lower excise than bottled wine. For most Australians, these are all points in its favour.

Johnny Farnham

Johnny Peter 'Farnesy' Farnham, Jr. AO (born 1 July 1949), is an English-born Australian pop singer. He later changed his stage name to John Farnham in an attempt to be taken more seriously, which should not be taken seriously.

Farnham was the last Englishman to be transported to Australia, having been forced to travel down under in an attempt to prevent him pursuing a singing career in his homeland, which would have sullied the 1960s heyday of the Beatles and the Rolling Stones. Following his arrival in Australia, Farnham went on to commit further heinous offences involving singing, acting, hairstyling, and the flagrant use of bagpipes in a power ballad.

Farnham looking characteristically pleased with himself. *Sean 917*

Despite his notoriety, Farnham is responsible for the most success-ful local album of all time, some of the most successful tours in the nation's history, and the mockery of Australian popular music in much of the world.

Early life

Farnham was born in Dagenham, England, a circumstance that later led to the Australian vernacular use of the word 'dag' to mean someone chronically uncool.

After sailing from the United Kingdom to become one of Australia's many unwanted boat people, Farnham went on to become a pop idol. His first single, 'Sadie (The Cleaning Lady)' made history as the first musical recording to be classed a crime against humanity by a Hague tribunal, but in its day sold more than 180,000 copies in Australia.* Farnham's ability to profit from telling a cleaner that she would never have a better job was an early sign that despite his relocation to class-free Australia, he would remain very much a Briton.

Building on the success of 'Sadie', Johnny Farnham was named King of Pop for five consecutive years from 1969, an achievement that led to him creating the Australian republican movement.

Farnham appeared on *Countdown*'s first colour episode in 1975, in which Skyhooks debuted their single 'Horror Movie'. The band wrote the song, with its famous lyric 'Horror movie right there on my TV', on learning that Farnham was to introduce them.

---

* Astonishingly, this is not a joke. Wikipedia says this made it the top-selling single in Australian history to that date, but surely it's an error.

Solo career

After his time with Little River Band made their sales significantly littler, Farnham resumed his solo career. Although his repertoire was as terrible as ever, so was most of the music of the mid-1980s, making him the perfect artist for the decade.

His 1986 album *Whispering Jack* became the most successful album by a local artist in Australia's history. Named after the singer—who, having failed to shake off 'Johnny', was now attempting to call himself 'Jack'—the album achieved its success despite Farnham bellowing on every song instead of whispering as promised. It was not the first time he would break a vow to his fans.

The record's iconic single, 'You're the Voice', made audio engineering history with the accuracy of its reproduction of the frenzied keening sounds made by a whale dying of asphyxiation. The single has been responsible for inducing tinnitus in hundreds of thousands of Australians, who were forced to play other music at high volumes to rid their suffering brains of this notorious earworm.

The single also hit the top ten in Germany, Switzerland and Austria, but then so did David Hasselhoff. More appropriately, its highest charting position in America was 82.

'You're the Voice' has nevertheless left a lasting and much valued legacy, as, since its release, no pop single has ever featured a bagpipe solo.*

In honour of his extraordinary chart success, Farnham was named the Australian of the Year of 1987, despite not even being an Australian national

---

* While this claim has not been tested, investigating whether it is true is not advised.

when the award was decided. He has faithfully remained 'of the year 1987' ever since.

Farnham followed his biggest album with *Age of Reason*, which referred nostalgically to the period before he became the biggest singer in the country. It was the biggest-selling album of 1988, and its follow-up, *Chain Reaction*, a tribute to the chemical process that rendered his trademark mullet blond and immobile, achieved the same feat in 1990.

John Farnham depicted in full terrifying flight at Melbourne's Walk of Stars. *Johan Fantenberg*

The singer was cast as the title character in a revival of *Jesus Christ Superstar* in 1992—a tribute to his career's extraordinary inability to remain dead.

Later touring years

Farnham spent November 2002 to June 2003 crossing the nation on his iconic 'The Last Time' tour. Many thousands of Australians attended purely to hear Johnny personally promise that he would never perform again.

Despite this undertaking, Johnny has conducted at least 167 subsequent national tours, including the 'Had My Fingers Crossed When I Said It Was The Last Time' tour, the 'Really Really Truly Last Time Except In The Event Anyone Wants More' tour, the 'Oh Look, They Did Want More!' tour, and the 'Might As Well Accept I'm Going To Be Doing This Until I Die And Even Afterwards If That's Somehow Feasible' tour.

Farnham's music will continue to be a part of our national life whenever Australians find themselves stuck in a taxi, and can't be bothered asking the driver to turn off Smooth FM.

Fast food in Australia

Australia's **fast food** operators are a combination of massive global chains and a few local ones bravely holding out against the American invaders. In recent years, some Australian chains have also found success by slavishly pretending to be Mexican or Portuguese.

Fast food chains have been a major contributor to Australia's world-class obesity epidemic, helping to transform Australians from a traditionally active, outdoors people to a nation of couch-dwelling slobs. In particular, the chains' partnerships with televised sport have helped to convince Australians that it's much more fun to watch fit people running around on TV than to exercise themselves.

These companies are also major employees of young Australians, whom they offer 'valuable real-world business experience'—earning minimum wage in return for making huge conglomerates even more profitable.

Major fast food chains

McDonald's—known for localising its burgers the world over, the local subsidiary's one concession to Australian tastes is the intermittently available McOz, which contains beetroot. The McOz has led customers to a far greater appreciation of the company's burgers that do not contain beetroot.

Australia also pioneered McCafé, the chain's attempt to encourage customers who don't want generic mass-produced burgers to consume generic mass-produced café food instead. The McCafé concept was an attempt to tap into the Starbucks market, the viability of which can be judged by Starbucks' closure of nearly all its Australian outlets.

Hungry Jack's—visitors to Australia are always surprised that here, Burger King uses its old logo with a weird name, born of a deal struck when Australia seemed even more of a parochial backwater than it is today. At one point, the Australian version came up against new stores branded 'Burger King', but the local chain's superior market knowledge enabled it to commit burger regicide. Its longtime slogan 'the burgers are better at Hungry Jack's' is the most accurate marketing posture of any fast food company, as it promises only that the burgers are better than McDonald's', as opposed to objectively good.

KFC—the Colonel's long association with Australian cricket has been criticised by public health experts, but perhaps the most bizarre aspect of the partnership has been KFC's attempts to encourage crowds to wear its fried chicken buckets upside down on their heads. The fact that many cricket attendees are willing to do so speaks to the volume of alcohol consumed at cricket matches.

Krispy Kreme—this visionary company, which figured out how to make donuts even more unhealthy by glazing them, is now ubiquitous in 7-Eleven's stores and petrol stations. This has made it possible for Australian motoring enthusiasts to have a donut and then do a donut.

Red Rooster—the local competitor to KFC serves chicken that's been roasted instead of deep fried. As this makes their product slightly less unhealthy, Red Rooster has struggled in the market.

Subway—the 'sandwich artists' have catered to Australian palates by offering smashed avocado, allowing Subway both to win over local customers and keep millennials out of the property market.

A rare image of a Red Rooster in the wild. *Bidgee*

Nando's—a Portuguese chicken chain that's actually South African.

Oporto—a Portuguese chicken chain that's actually Australian. There are no Portuguese Portuguese chicken chains in Australia.

Guzman y Gomez—a Mexican chain that's actually an Australian chain, named after two kindly Mexican gentlemen who don't exist. It has prospered despite serving its burritos with a salsa of lies.

Pizza Hut—this venerable company's local operations nearly went broke in the 1990s after offering an all-you-can-eat deal that significantly underestimated its Australian customers' willingness to embrace obesity in return for cheap pizza.

Domino's—a pizza delivery company whose longtime slogan 'I've got the hots for what's in the box with the dots' was runner-up in the Cannes Advertising Festival's tortuous puns category to Sidchrome's 'You canna hand a man a grander spanner'.

Eagle Boys—a once-thriving business that ultimately foundered due to overestimating the demand for a pizza chain named after the villains in the Scrooge McDuck cartoons.*

Starbucks—after rapidly expanding across the country, the Seattle coffee chain belatedly realised that Australian consumers weren't interested in paying more for inferior coffee served in absurdly large cups. Only a few branches remain, in city areas where they appeal to tourists and international students who prefer Frappuccinos loaded with whipped cream and topping. In recent years, the chain has dropped 'Coffee' from its name, realising that it's not their strong suit.

First Fleet

A scheme to punish British criminals by forcing them to live in a more beautiful place with a better climate.

Flag of Australia

The **flag of Australia** was selected by King Edward VII in 1903, and displays all of the profound insight into Australia's distinctive national character that one would expect from someone who never visited Australia.

Nevertheless, the flag successfully represents modern Australia in that it's a mishmash of bits and pieces found elsewhere, with no recognition of the land's original inhabitants.

---

* I know they're technically the Beagle Boys but, honestly, this is the best explanation for the name I can think of.

The Australian flag is recognised as a symbol of the nation except in the primary context in which such symbols still have meaning: the sporting arena. Here, Australian national teams wear green and gold, to avoid being confused with almost every other nation's red, white and blue.

The long-running debate over changing the flag's design to a design that's less abjectly subservient to the United Kingdom has continued for some decades but, due to the Australian political system's general inability to resolve any question of identity or symbolism, no vote has been taken. Furthermore, the current flag remains popular with the bogan and redneck communities, who choose to express their deep affection and respect for the flag, and the homeland that it represents, by wearing it as a cape while they get pissed and shout abuse at passers-by.

Most political scientists now agree that it would be easier if another indifferent ruler simply picked a new flag.

Design

Technically, the flag is what vexillologists* refer to as a 'hotchpotch', 'jumble' or 'badly designed mess'.

It consists of three disparate elements, two of which appear on several other flags. In the upper canton, or dominant position, is the Union Jack, showing Britain's dominance over Australia, which has been maintained to the present day only in the fields of tea consumption and high-quality period dramas.

---

* That is, people who study flags, rather than people who are vexing, although such people are generally both.

Alternate national flag of Australia.

The Union Jack is itself a hotchpotch, made up of the flags of the United Kingdom, but it's expected that the British national flag will soon be simplified, when Scotland leaves the UK following Brexit.

The Southern Cross—or Crux, as it's known to none of the kind of people who tattoo it on their bodies—is commonly considered to be a symbol of Australia by people who are ignorant of the fact that it also appears on the flags of New Zealand, Brazil, Papua New Guinea, Samoa, and some regions of Argentina and Chile. Otherwise, however, it's uniquely Australian.

The final element is a seven-pointed star that was originally known as the Commonwealth Star, but today symbolises the Faith of the Seven in *Game of Thrones*. It represents the original six states, with one spare just in case New Zealand decides to join after all.

This star, along with the red centres of the stars on the flag of our trans-Tasman neighbour, are the only differences between the two countries' flags. This would be an easy way to distinguish between the two were Australia not famous for its Red Centre.

Nevertheless, the two flags are rarely confused in practice, as very few people have heard of New Zealand.

The Australian national flag is, however, confusingly similar to the Victorian state flag, which omits the Commonwealth Star, and has a crown above the Southern Cross for those who felt that having only the Union Jack wasn't quite subservient enough.

Frank Forde

Francis Michael 'Poor old Frank' Forde (18 July 1890–28 January 1983) was prime minister of Australia for eight days, which, to put it into perspective, is 20 per cent less time than Anthony Scaramucci was White House Communications Director.*

This was because, as deputy, he was sworn in the day after John Curtin's death, but lost a leadership ballot to Ben Chifley a week later, despite not having been behind in a single Newspoll. Thereafter, Forde returned patiently and rather pathetically to the deputy's role.

Ironically, his parliamentary career was extremely long. He spent five-and-a-half years in the Queensland legislative assembly before his 24 years as the federal member for Capricornia. After that, he served a further two-and-a-half years in the Queensland assembly, following a term as the high commissioner to Canada. Forde is the only person ever to bother returning to a state legislature after serving as Australia's national leader.

---

*   By the time of printing, readers no doubt will have forgotten him, as his tenure was brief even by Trumpian standards—he was the one who was sacked after an obscenity-laden interview with a journalist from *The New Yorker*.

Consequently, Forde was prime minister for eight of his roughly 11,600 days in political office, or approximately 0.06 per cent.

At his final state election in 1957, Ford lost his seat by just one vote. He disputed the result, leading to a by-election in which he was defeated by over four hundred votes. Had he won, he would most likely have become the state's Labor leader, before presumably getting dumped a week later.

Forde died in 1983, and was given a state funeral, which lasted for nearly as long as his time as PM—but this grand commemoration was almost completely overshadowed by Bob Hawke's election as federal ALP leader the very same day. Indeed, it was at his funeral that Senator John Button told Bill Hayden that he should resign.

One might conclude that Frank Forde was Australia's unluckiest politician, but even there, he misses out to Harold Holt.

Frente!

Frente! were one of Australia's best-known bands of the 1990s, despite their song 'Accidently [*sic**] Kelly Street'.

Fortunately, the rest of Frente!'s only full-length album is a collection of uniformly high-quality folk-pop that rewards a listen. Unfortunately, its name is *Marvin The Album*.

---

* Apparently the misspelling was accidental, but then they decided to keep it—a bad decision, but very much in keeping with the song itself.

Governor-General

The **Governor-General of the Commonwealth of Australia**, or **G-G**, is the monarch's representative, and appointed on the advice of the prime minister, whom they may also sack, in a sensible, stable arrangement that couldn't possibly result in any problems.

They are styled 'His/Her Excellency the Honourable', a customary title that does not require any evidence of actual excellence or honour.

Like the monarch, a governor-general is supposed to remain politically neutral, except when actively conspiring with the leader of the opposition to dismiss the incumbent government and install the opposition leader as acting prime minister.

The vice-regal office does not make a governor-general the head of state in technical terms, but unless British monarchs become considerably more interested in Australia, governors-general* will continue to serve essentially the same purpose. In particular, any legislation passed by the parliament must receive the governor-general's assent before becoming a law. This step is essentially automatic in practice, in keeping with the quaint and charming but conceptually terrifying lack of allowance for disasters that is the standard British approach to their unwritten constitutional arrangements.

In one sense, this is fortunate, as the rights guaranteed to the governor-general's office by the Australian constitution would produce riots in the street if they were ever actually used. Then again, the governor-general could quell said riots, as commander-in-chief of the military.

---

* This plural form is a particular favourite of Australian pedants.

In effect, the office possesses more than enough constitutional power for the governor-general to function as a kind of dictator, so it is fortunate indeed that all those appointed to the office have been remarkably sensible and restrained in the exercise of their responsibilities, except for that one guy.

The winner of the Great Australian Sack Race of 1975. *T. & R. Annan & Sons Ltd*

Many republicans favour the replacement of the governor-general with an elected president holding a similar ceremonial office with the same powers. As this would give the Australian president the legitimacy of being directly elected, unlike the prime minister, who isn't even mentioned in the constitution, and the president would have the power to reject laws, dismiss parliaments and call in troops, it's quite possible that this step would make Britain's politely optimistic constitutional conventions seem sensible by contrast.

Great Barrier Reef

The former **Great Barrier Reef** was the world's largest coral reef system. Once teeming with life, it stretched for 2300 kilometres off the coast of Queensland. Named one of the seven natural wonders of the world, and listed as a World Heritage Site in 1981, it was the largest structure ever constructed by living organisms.

Still, it'll grow back eventually.

Pauline Hanson

Pauline Lee Hanson (née **Seccombe**, formerly **Zagorski**, currently **Pariah**), is an Australian politician who was born on 27 May 1954 and reborn at the 2016 federal election. She is the founder of Pauline Hanson's One Nation, a growing political force that welcomes all who subscribe to Australian values, aren't the wrong sort of ethnic and never forget whose name appears right there in the name of the party.

Hanson became famous throughout Australia and infamous throughout the Asia–Pacific for her fiery 1996 maiden speech in which she attacked Asians. In recent years, however, she has reinvented herself for the new century and started attacking Muslims instead. Her opposition to Asian Muslims has remained consistent throughout.

Over the years, many have dismissed Hanson as an extremist xeno-phobe who inhabits the political fringe. She has been unable to shake this perception, perhaps because, as she once revealed during a television interview, she didn't know what xenophobia was.* Hanson now claims that this was a misrepresentation, as she has never feared Nick Xenophon.

Early life and career

Hanson's parents ran a fish and chip shop in Ipswich. It's not known whether they vaccinated the young Pauline, or whether she instead benefited from the herd immunity she would later work so hard to undermine.

---

* Her response during that interview, 'Please explain?' has become something of a trademark, perhaps because she also doesn't quite understand the meaning of irony.

Even as a teenager, Hanson displayed the inclinations that would later fuel her political career, demanding that the shop avoid special treatment for those fish varieties that were exclusive to Australian waters, and refuse to allow salmon, tuna or any other non-white fish to 'swamp' varieties like flake. The young Pauline always preferred to consume her fish and chips uncooked, as the deep fryer made them less white.

Hanson pictured at a bookshop, shortly before trying to close it down. *Velovotee*

Hanson's first involvement in political life came when she was elected to Ipswich City Council in 1994, after campaigning against the funding of a new library. This principled stance against knowledge has been a hallmark of her political platform ever since.

In 1996, she joined the Liberal Party, and was endorsed as its candidate for the seat of Oxley, the safest Labor seat in Queensland. But even though she was disendorsed over a letter she wrote to the *Queensland Times* warning about 'reverse racism' towards Aborigines, she was nevertheless successful in winning the seat,* as voters were too busy evicting Keating's Labor to worry who they were installing instead.

Alternatively, Oxley voters may have been perfectly comfortable with Hanson's views on race, but that conclusion is best avoided, as it involves negative stereotypes of people based on where they come from.

---

* Despite the disendorsement, she still appeared as a Liberal on the ballot paper, because reprinting the papers was apparently more problematic than a major party candidate saying something that caused widespread outrage and feelings of revulsion among her prospective colleagues.

Maiden speech

Hanson's maiden speech warned about the perils of the 'Asianisation' of Australia, and how disruptive it would prove to 'our' way of life. This rang true to many Australians, who have long endured the significant changes wrought by Asian migration, such as increased access to bubble tea, yum cha and karaoke.

Hanson also criticised the special treatment given to Aboriginal people merely because they happened to have been subjected to genocide. She argued it was unfair that she was unable to enjoy programs designed to benefit Aboriginal people purely because she wasn't one.

The first-term MP also objected to the notion that Australia was Aboriginal land—a notion rejected by Australian property law in all but the most limited cases—dramatically asking 'Where the hell do I go?' After the speech, there was no shortage of people who were willing to tell her.

The speech made headlines throughout the region, and even though Hanson was by this point an independent MP with no role in the government, her strident anti-immigration platform was given effect, as many Asians declined to visit or study in Australia as a result of her comments. This helped to move Australia towards Hanson's vision of being One Nation undisturbed by tourist and education income from its economic powerhouse neighbours.*

---

* The enduring success of Hanson's anti-Asian campaign is perhaps best illustrated by the fact that her former fish and chip shop is now run by people with Vietnamese heritage.

Incarceration

In 1998, Tony Abbott set up the Australians for Honest Politics Trust, to try to bring down One Nation and Hanson by initiating civil cases, while trickily keeping his involvement secret.

The strategy ultimately worked too well—Hanson was jailed for election funding irregularities in 2003. This led to a huge increase in public sympathy towards her that only grew when her conviction was set aside on appeal, bolstering her trademark claim of persecution by the elites with uncharacteristically convincing evidence.

Abbott learned from this experience that it is better to co-opt the policies of the far right than to seek to exclude them, while Hanson's treatment in this situation remains the only legitimate one of her many grievances.

Election to Senate

Before 2016, Hanson's only election to public office had been with the word 'Liberal' beside her name on the ballot—after the foundation of One Nation, she unsuccessfully ran for office on multiple occasions in Queensland and New South Wales. A tradition emerged of her comeback being mooted early on election night, only to be followed by an eventual narrow loss.

This strategy of narrowly missing out proved a solid earner for Hanson, who managed to receive substantial public election funding on the basis of her strong primary votes, without the inconvenience of doing any representing.

This mutually satisfactory arrangement ended after she and three colleagues were elected to the Senate in the 2016 election. Had it not been a double dissolution election, only Hanson would have been elected, meaning that One Nation would not have been recognised as an official party—not unlike when several of its key figures went to jail.

Instead, One Nation achieved party status, and became the Senate crossbench's most reliably cross element.

Policy positions

Hanson is known for her commitment to protectionism, and she is particularly determined to maintain strong barriers against foreign ideas like tolerance and universal human rights. However, she is sympathetic to the wholesale import of ideas popularised by Donald Trump, including explicit support for Vladimir Putin.

Hanson is even more committed to protectionism regarding her role as head of her party, which has no mechanisms for internal democracy. This reflects Hanson's scepticism about elections, given her decades of difficulties with them.

Consequently, Hanson's control over One Nation is the envy of major party leaders, and one former leader still regrets his colleagues' rejection of his attempt to rename their party 'Tony Abbott's Liberals'.

Nowadays, Hanson has become a pioneer in the emerging policy area of Islamophobia. The One Nation leader has long argued against halal certification, eager to help Australian companies save money on what she claims is an excessively expensive approval process, in return for the small inconvenience of guaranteeing that hundreds of thousands of potential customers can't consume their products.

Hanson's party is generally tough on law and order issues, except when it comes to leaders of political parties who have been locked up for a simple misunderstanding. The party has also been known for its support of a flat tax, which has the distinct advantage of being a policy that the party's members and leaders can easily understand, if not articulate.

One Nation is also firmly against action on climate change, and its members recently swam out to the Great Barrier Reef to prove to the media that the stories about coral bleaching had been greatly exaggerated, bolstering their case considerably by choosing a location that wasn't part of the hundreds of kilometres affected by coral bleaching. They have since revised their position, arguing that there's nothing wrong with things turning white.

Some One Nation state candidates have accused the 'gays' of using Nazi mind control techniques—in which case, the techniques are clearly ineffective, since same-sex marriage remains illegal. In any event, by making these accusations, they have made it abundantly clear that many One Nation candidates' minds are entirely impenetrable.

Despite its maverick reputation, fringe policy positions and anti-establishment image, One Nation votes with the government nearly all of the time, allowing its voters to strike a potent theoretical blow against the status quo in Australian politics while supporting it in practice.

One Nation associates

Rodney Culleton—still a duly elected senator for Western Australia, although only in his own mind,* Culleton has the distinction of being the

---

* And on Twitter, where he remains @senatorculleton as of the time of writing.

first member of parliament to require the High Court to decide which of two competing ineligibilities rendered him unable to retain his seat.

While Culleton's career in the Senate may have been brief, and characterised by frequent absences in order to defend himself in multiple proceedings, his service will never be forgotten by all those who study Australian constitutional law or enjoy reading amusing court transcripts.*

Peter Georgiou—Culleton's brother-in-law assumed his seat after it was declared vacant, leading to one of the more awkward Christmas lunches in family history.

Malcolm Roberts—also known as '**Malcolm-Ieuan: Roberts., the living soul**', when writing crank letters to prime ministers,† is a self-declared and -taught climate expert who is more credible and capable of interpreting simple 'empirical evidence' than all the world's thousands of recognised climate scientists put together, according to the one reputable source: Roberts.

He and/or his living soul attended Donald Trump's inauguration after pressuring the Australian embassy into getting him invited. At the time of writing, questions are being asked about his dual citizenship status—questions that were not satisfactorily resolved by the claim that he was choosing to believe he was not a UK citizen.

---

* Culleton's statements in his own defence have been compared with *The Castle*, but, as they're real, his arguments are even more entertaining than Dennis Denuto's.

† Roberts once wrote 'The Woman, Julia-Eileen: Gillard., acting as The Honourable JULIA EILEEN GILLARD' a letter that claimed he was not liable for the carbon tax because he had never been presented with any 'material facts of evidence that compels me . . . to be a member of a society and believe that none exist', among other equally idiosyncratic reasons.

Brian Burston—currently one of the least overtly controversial One Nation senators, he has a long history with the party. In his maiden speech, Burston protested that the rights of white Australians to celebrate their unique culture were being oppressed by the dictatorship of multiculturalism, a delightfully retro nod to the white pride and instinctive objections to racial diversity that led to Pauline Hanson's initial break with the Liberal Party.

David Oldfield—a former staffer of Tony Abbott who threw his support behind Hanson after her maiden speech, he successfully rode her coat tails to eight years in the NSW Upper House, something that Hanson herself proved unable to achieve on several occasions. He split with Hanson's party in 2000, after which his Legislative Council membership meant that he was able to register One Nation NSW, a separate entity from the federal party, meaning that there were two One Nations.

Oldfield was a radio presenter for many years, but now spews forth his Islamophobia on a freelance basis. He was once a contestant on *Celebrity Survivor*—regrettably, he survived.

David Ettridge—the other of the 'two Davids' who were once Hanson's lieutenants, he was there in the 'good old days', having been jailed for electoral fraud alongside Hanson.

James Ashby—a former staffer for Peter Slipper, Ashby has found even more power, and less personal controversy, further to the right as Hanson's chief of staff, as gay men apparently constitute one of the few minority groups of which Pauline Hanson isn't actively suspicious. Ashby has become the latest man to be perceived by a sexist media as the puppetmaster behind Hanson's success, and will probably be dumped in the near future after a messy falling-out, like all the others.

Bob Hawke

Robert James Lee 'Bob' 'Hawkie' Hawke (born 9 December 1929) is an Australian politician and folk icon, embodying such traditional larrikin values as joking, drinking and philandering.

Hawkie served as prime minister of Australia from 1983 to 1991, the longest period that any Labor prime minister has survived before undergoing the now-traditional departure process of being torn down by colleagues.

Unlike most Australian leaders, Hawke did not have a patrician establishment background—his prolonged electoral success is proof that in Australian democracy, anyone can become prime minister, as long as they have world-record-level ability at skolling beer.

Hawkie's success reflected a brief flowering of the notion that the best bloke in Australia ought to run it, a principle later abandoned for the current system of briefly tolerating the leader whom the electorate dislikes less than their opponent.

Early life and family

Unlike most prime ministers, Hawke has deep roots across much of the country*, having been born in South Australia, educated in Western Australia and Canberra, worked in Melbourne, retired to New South Wales, and generally behaved like a Queenslander.

Hawke was born in Bordertown, South Australia, an ideal location from which to quickly leave the state and never look back. At the age of 15,

---

* As opposed to rooting across much of the country, which he is also understood to have accomplished.

he boasted to his school friends in Perth that he would become prime minister someday, an early sign of the supreme self-confidence that would take him all the way to the top, and then inspire his colleagues to bring him back down again.

The future prime minister married Hazel Masterson in 1956 at Perth's Trinity Church, a fitting location to formalise a relationship that, before long, would have three participants, as Hawke began his relationship with Blanche D'Alpuget in 1976 after she proved to be the only other person in Australia who was as interested in Hawke as he was, ultimately producing two biographies of him.

A yard glass—a ridiculous thing to drink from both in quantity and form. *PeteVerdon*

Education

Hawke won a Rhodes Scholarship in 1952 after convincing the judges that he certainly thought of himself as a future leader. He attended University College Oxford, and graduated with a Bachelor of Letters degree after writing a thesis on wage fixing in Australia. This proved a brilliant choice, since none of his British examiners knew anything about wage fixing in Australia, and decided simply to pass him so that they weren't required to read up on it.

During his time at Oxford, Hawke set a world record for drinking beer, downing two-and-a-half imperial pints (1.4 litres), equivalent to a yard of ale, in 11 seconds. This record has never been beaten, largely because nobody outside Oxford has used yards to measure beer since the 12th century.

It is postulated that no student will ever beat Hawke's record unless they are equally eager to find an escape from writing a thesis about wage fixing in Australia.

Hawke was forced to drink the yard glass during a college dinner as part of a traditional Oxford penalty imposed by the 'sconce master'. He was the first student in University College history to realise that deliberately accruing these penalties also meant accruing free beer.

On returning to Australia, Hawke enrolled in a doctorate at the Australian National University, writing about arbitration law. He later abandoned the degree, correctly concluding that it would be simpler and less tedious to become prime minister and simply change arbitration law, rather than having to write 100,000 words about the current regime.

Australian Council of Trade Unions

Shortly after beginning work at the ACTU, Hawke won a 15-shilling increase in the national wage from the Conciliation and Arbitration Commission. This victory began his process of accruing considerable public acclaim, a relic of a very different Australia where trade unions were popular, and their leaders seen as crusaders for the good of workers, rather than for unlimited credit cards.

Hawke was elected ACTU president on a modernising platform, and, radically for unionists of the day, declined to describe himself as a socialist. He became known as a negotiator and pragmatist, and his novel approach of delivering tangible improvements rather than rhetoric made him not only the most popular ACTU leader of all time, but the only popular ACTU leader of all time.

In 1979, while also serving as the ALP's federal president, he had an alcohol-related physical collapse. This led him to undertake the first of his trademark tearful *mea culpa* television interviews, in which he promised to beat his alcoholism, successfully turning potential scandal into public sympathy.

Subsequent polls showed that Hawke was more popular than both the prime minister, Malcolm Fraser, and the Labor leader, Bill Hayden, proving that Australian voters view political experience as significantly less important than drinking prowess.*

Political career

Hawke stood for the safe Melbourne seat of Wills in 1980, winning comfortably. Hayden installed him as shadow industrial relations minister, after which Hawke immediately began a shadowy campaign of workplace destabilisation, encouraged by polls showing that he would win an election if he were the leader.

---

* This is why by 2025, David Boon will be prime minister.

Ultimately, in 1983, Hayden resigned to let the more electable man take on Fraser, acknowledging that he had no chance of winning a popularity contest against a guy with a beer-drinking world record.

The PM had called a snap election on the same day, hoping to strike before Labor's leadership tensions had been resolved, but, in this instance, Fraser's shock collusion with a governor-general was unable to deny Labor.

Prime minister

After inflicting the heaviest of the very few defeats in the Coalition's history, Hawke was sworn in as the 23rd prime minister of Australia on 11 March 1983. Upon assuming office, he immediately announced that the Fraser government's misrepresentation of the budget situation meant that he wouldn't be able to proceed with many of his election promises, beginning a tradition that continues to this day upon every change of government.

Hawke in 1987, before his smile was wiped off by Paul Keating.
Department of Foreign Affairs and Trade website—www.dfat.gov.au

Before long, Hawke and his treasurer, Paul Keating, began a comprehensive reform program, deregulating the economy, floating the dollar, and imposing dramatic reductions in many areas, most notably the size of the swimwear in which Hawke was regularly photographed.

Hawke reintroduced Gough Whitlam's Medibank scheme as Medicare, having noted that 'care' and 'bank' are antithetical to most Australians.

He also guaranteed that this would remain the case by selling off the publicly owned Commonwealth Bank.

He also introduced a fringe benefits tax, despite never allowing his own hair to appear in anything less than a voluminous bouffant.*

Setting a precedent followed by all subsequent Labor PMs, Hawke quickly abandoned the party's industrial base when in office, hobnobbing instead with the likes of the entrepreneur Sir Peter Abeles. During the pilots' strike of 1989, he took the side of those workers who were serving as airline CEOs, offering public funds to help them through the crisis. A decade later, this former union leader's actions would provide a useful template for the Howard government's union-busting efforts on the waterfront.

At his campaign launch in 1987, Hawke made a famous promise that no child in Australia would live in poverty by 1990. While this was never achieved, his failure helped ensure that no Hawke would live in the Lodge by 1991.

Removal

Hawke's string of election victories had been greatly assisted by the civil war between the unelectably dull John Howard (as he then seemed), and the unelectably flashy Andrew Peacock (as he still seems). The short-lived 'Joh for Canberra' campaign, which asserted that the rest of the country would get behind a peanut-peddling National Party despot whose victories in Queensland resulted from massive gerrymandering, also helped Hawke stay on top.

---

* This is a terrible pun, but Hawke's hairstyle was perhaps the most notable thing about the man—and there are many notable things about the man.

By 1990, the Coalition had chosen the economist Dr John Hewson as opposition leader. Although his tenure is now remembered as the reason why oppositions should not present detailed economic plans to the electorate before taking office, Hewson's comprehensive 'Fightback!' reform package blindsided Hawke, who was used to his most economically savvy opponent being Paul Keating.

After he eventually replaced Hawke, Keating famously described the 1993 election as the sweetest victory of them all, but those who know him well say that he enjoyed his victory over his former boss even more.

Legacy

Despite their long-running personal enmity, Hawke and Keating presided over what is now recognised by both sides of politics as a visionary and much-needed program of reform. Their ongoing media bickering is yet to entirely undermine their inextricably linked legacy.

In the decades since he left politics, Hawke has been the most popular living former Australian prime minister by a considerable distance. There are several reasons for this—first, his competition consists of Paul Keating, John Howard, Kevin Rudd, Julia Gillard and Tony Abbott; and, second, he makes an annual appearance at the cricket to skoll a beer.

Lleyton Hewitt

Lleyton Glynn Hewitt is Australia's last tennis player to win multiple grand slam singles titles, and became the youngest male player ever to reach number one, at age 20, and then one of the youngest to lose the title, never to regain it. His career was a microcosm of the spirit of Australian tennis, in that he achieved incredible feats in his early days, and then spent a very long time failing to replicate them.

As a player, Hewitt coupled the intensity and powder-keg temperament of a young John McEnroe with the inadequate serve of Rafael Nadal with a back injury. He was renowned for a never-say-die attitude that saw him fighting until the very end, chasing down balls that other players would sensibly have abandoned in order to conserve their strength for the next point.

He was especially known for his signature offensive topspin lob, and also for his signature offensive slurs hurled at opponents and umpires alike.

Hewitt was unusually in sync with his audience, frequently shouting 'Come on!' at himself exactly when frustrated viewers wanted to do the same thing. He was also famous for celebrating his opponent's unforced

Hewitt characteristically wore his cap backwards, leading some observers to wonder if he knew how it worked. *Carine06*

errors, leading to significant debate about whether he was excessively competitive or just unpleasant.

Hewitt won the US Open in 2001 at the age of 20, and Wimbledon the following year, leading to hopes that he would be the next Australian champion to dominate the sport for years, in the manner of Laver and Newcombe. Instead, he tanked after two grand slams, in the manner of Rafter. His only subsequent grand slam final was the Australian Open in 2005, when he became the Aussie player whose margin of failure to win his home grand slam was the most frustratingly narrow since Pat Cash's bicentennial loss in 1988.

This was to be his last appearance in a grand slam final, but he remained on the tour for another 11 years of diminishing returns, and also serves.

Personal life

Hewitt was engaged to the Belgian tennis star Kim Clijsters, who became popular with local crowds and was christened 'Aussie Kim' as a result of the relationship. The nickname is fitting in another sense, in that she, unlike her ex, has won the Australian Open.

Shortly after losing his only Australian Open singles final, he proposed to *Home and Away* star Bec Cartwright, a fitting consolation prize. Since their marriage, in 2005, they have been very happy together and shared everything, including the gradual decline of both their careers.

Post-tennis career

Hewitt was part of Channel Seven's Australian Open commentary team for the last five years of his tennis career, and remains so today. It is understood that he originally began commentating because he recognised it was his best chance of featuring in another final.

Despite his controversies, Hewitt's career deserves to be recognised as outstanding. He managed through sheer determination to remain the best player in the world for 80 weeks, which is approximately 80 weeks longer than his natural talent warranted. But perhaps most extraordinary of all is the fact that he made it to number one for any weeks when he was born in the same year as Roger Federer.

Despite his pugnacious 'Aussie battler' image, Hewitt was in fact a resident of the Bahamas for much of his career. Regardless of how he was perceived elsewhere, he will always be remembered as one of the all-time greats of Bahamian tennis.

Hey Hey It's Saturday

Hey Hey It's Saturday, also known as *Hey Hey*, *Hey Hey It's Saturday Except It's Wednesday*, and *Oh No It's Hey Hey*, is the most unlikely success in the history of international television. It ran from 1971 to 1999, except in 1978, when co-hosts Oswald Q* Ostrich and that puppet presented a game show on Network Ten. They lost, and so had to return to Nine and their original format.

Eventually broadcast in prime time on Saturday night, *Hey Hey* benefited from an era before cable television, the internet and VCRs, when people

---

* Wikipedia insists this middle initial exists, confirming its status as the greatest repository of human knowledge ever created, but is silent on what it stands for. Perhaps 'Quiet, Daryl'?

had more limited options. In its heyday, or Hey Heyday, families were obliged either to watch one of the shows the four national networks served up, leave the house, or talk to each other.

Faced with these options, they overwhelmingly chose *Hey Hey*, whose variety format meant that even when one segment wasn't especially enjoyable, a different unenjoyable segment was only a few minutes away.

Origins

In its earliest days, *Hey Hey It's Saturday* was a cartoon program in which Daryl Somers and his ostrich co-host riffed between cartoon episodes. In those days, audience research techniques were highly primitive, which led the network to mistakenly conclude that the audience were tuning in for the hilarious banter between the two co-hosts, instead of the cartoons.

Development

As the show evolved, its audience warmed to its format of Carroll and voice-over man John Blackman constantly interrupting and mocking the hapless Somers, as viewers quickly found themselves wanting to do the same thing. Somers proved so ideal a target for his colleagues' humiliation that the show endured in this form for many years.

There were also various female co-hosts throughout the series, one of whom was known as 'Ding Dong', and another of whom was afforded an even lower status. None of the female hosts was ever allowed to have the same screen time given to a puppet made of felt.

Ham dressed as hot dog . . . *Hey Hey*'s hi-jinks have not necessarily stood the test of time.

Regular segments

Red Faces—a talent show in which awful contestants would perform, after a fashion, before being gonged off by Red Symons. Sheer relief at their departure generally enticed the two guest judges to give higher marks than the only accurate assessor, Red.

Chook Lotto—a parody of televised lottery programs where the numbers were written on frozen chickens instead of balls. That's all.

Plucka Duck—after belatedly realising that 'Chook Lotto' wasn't very good, the team replaced the segment with an equally banal game show featuring someone dressed as a duck.

Molly's Melodrama—music industry legend Ian 'Molly' Meldrum's perpetual enthusiasm for the latest hits from Australia and abroad was constantly interrupted by thinly veiled references to his sexuality.

Meldrum was originally invited to participate because of his iconic status in Australian television, but was kept on because his propensity to mumble made Somers' presenting shine by contrast.

Magic Word—basically the board game Balderdash, with a different name for copyright purposes.

Media Watch—basically *Media Watch*, if *Media Watch* focused exclusively on unfunny typos.

Celebrity Head—an example of the show's use of double entendre that sucked, this guessing game has since become a time-wasting staple for Australians stuck in airports.

The Great Aussie Joke—a segment where Shane Bourne and Maurie Fields would tell jokes sent in by viewers. This was included so that each episode of *Hey Hey* would contain at least one genuine joke, thus rendering the program eligible for the comedy category at the Logies.

Reunion

The show was brought back for two 'specials' in 2009, although there was nothing special about them. The decision to revisit old 'favourite' pieces of content backfired when Harry Connick Jr pointed out that a sketch featuring performers in blackface might have been a tad ill-advised.*

Despite the Nine Network explicitly warning that a strong ratings performance could lead to its permanent return, enough viewers foolhardily tuned in for it to be given two ten-week runs in 2010.

---

* It was so cringe-inducing, in fact, that it doesn't feel appropriate to put a joke here.

Despite its subsequent re-cancellation, Somers regularly promises the show's imminent return.* In the meantime, old episodes can be viewed at the website heyhey.tv for $59.95†, which is considerably less cheap than the jokes.

Hills hoist

The **Hills hoist** is as common in the Australian backyard as half-rusted beer cans and bindi-eyes. It's the perfect clothes-drying device for anyone who has plenty of space and no interest in aesthetics, leading to the device's ubiquity in suburban homes.

As well as being used for drying clothes, Hills hoists are frequently used as a handy carousel by children with sufficiently long arms.

The Hills hoist originated in Adelaide, which is also surrounded by grass and a chore. Hills hoists are still made in South Australia, where they rank as one of the state's most famous exports besides wine, and people relocating to Melbourne.

Scientists believe that, long after the human race has died out, Hills hoists will survive as a monument to the civilisation that once existed across the Australian continent. Some historians have hypothesised that future alien visitors will wonder why so many Hills hoists have empty cask wine bladders tied to them.‡

---

* Most recently in 2016, as of going to print. Yes, last year.
† Per year rather than each—but still!
‡ Unless those future historians are lucky enough to have access to Wikipedia, and consult the entry for 'Goon of Fortune'.

Holden

Holden is an Australian automobile manufacturer, though not a manufacturer of Australian automobiles for much longer, and nor has it ever ultimately been Australian. Nevertheless, Holden is as much of an Aussie icon as Don Lane, Mel Gibson and Terri Irwin.

Origins

In 1852, James Alexander Holden came to Australia and established a saddlery business—the only occasion when Holden offered leather seats as standard. In 1931, General Motors bought what was by then a car body producer, and it began producing cars for the local market in 1948. As such, Holden has never produced a car that was Australian designed, manufactured and owned. Nevertheless, Holden has long been the least un-Australian of all the un-Australian cars sold on the local market.

Dominance

Following the FX, which was the first 'Australian' car, the FJ Holden became an Australian institution from 1953 and was followed by the FE, FC and FB. By 1958, the company had more than half the domestic market, and pioneered the utility for farmers and tradesmen, and the Monaro for a sector of Australian society that reached its apex in the 1970s, the bogan.

In the 1970s, Holden had the famous slogan 'football, meat pies, kangaroos and Holden cars'—a uniquely Australian rewrite of GM's uniquely American slogan 'baseball, hot dogs, apple pies and Chevrolets'. This trumpeting of Holden's local identity coincided with a move away from local designs to tweaked GM international models like Vauxhall, Opel and Chevrolet. In many cases, the only thing that was uniquely Australian about the cars was their rebadging under a worse name, like Torana, Cascada, Frontera or Scurry.

The longest-lasting Holden marque was the Commodore, which shared its name with another plasticky, tape-playing American product that was popular in the 1980s, the Commodore 64. Also like the Commodore 64, Holden was to lose significant market share to Japanese competitors.

Decline

By 2006, Holden had slumped to less than 16 per cent of the Australian car market, and had started to sell designs like the Aussie-only Barina, originally a Daewoo, making it a Korean-American-Australian car. While its cars were increasingly foreign-sourced, Holden was arguably more Australian than ever, thanks to massive infusions of government money. The Rudd government gave $149 million to build a localised version of the Chevrolet Cruze, but this was ultimately as successful an Australian import as 'our' Tom Cruise.

The Gillard government, along with the SA and Victorian state governments, gave Holden a further $270 million lifeline in 2012, in return for which the company decided, just one year later, to cease vehicle manufacturing in Australia. Holden's Australian factory did, however, endure longer than the Gillard government.

Holden's departure will lead to the loss of just under three thousand jobs, but the company has been eager to stress that it will continue to maintain a dealership network in Australia, making the company as Australian as BMW.

Holden's new approach is merely an evolution of what GM has done since the 1930s—selling cars in Australia, under an 'Australian' brand, and taking the profits overseas. Local jobs will remain, but only so that the Australians on the ground can tally up just how much money is being sent to America.

Future

Holden will maintain its brand and famous lion logo, which, like the company, is not discernibly Australian. The image of a lion rolling a stone is supposed to refer to the apocryphal story of how humans discovered the wheel. For Holden, it will aptly represent a wheel being rolled off an overseas production line by non-Australian creatures.

While the iconic Australian car company is entering its most un-Australian phase, most experts nevertheless expect Holden to maintain its proud legacy of being the car company Australians choose when they can't afford European, are a bit too prejudiced to buy Asian, and haven't got a Ford dealership nearby.

John Howard

John Winston Howard, more widely known as **Little Johnny**, defied the odds, the critics, his colleagues and his own personality to become Australia's second-longest-serving prime minister. He did so by refusing to accept that his political career was finished, despite repeatedly being told so by colleagues and voters alike.

As a result of what seemed like fool- ish persistence, Howard went on to become one of the most dominant prime ministers in Australian history, as well as the most submissive in terms of relations with the US and UK.

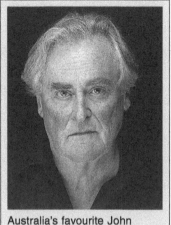

Australia's favourite John Howard. *Theresa Sarjeant*

Arriving in office after 13 years of Labor, he swept to power using the slogan 'For all of us', conveniently not clarifying that 'us' meant the Liberal Party and its big business supporters. He set out to reverse many of the signature social reforms of the Hawke–Keating period, although he did retain its most distinctive element—a capable treasurer who was perpetually angling for his boss's job.

Howard's rigid, nostalgic, insular vision for Australia lay in stark contrast to the lush, verdant, expanse of the eyebrows for which he is renowned. Assisted by his 'battlers'—voters in outer-suburban seats who were mort- gaged to the hilt and cared for little besides their precious houses and the refugees and/or banks who might steal them—Howard's electoral position was impregnable for a decade.

Ironically, he was eventually undone by his greatest triumph, a fourth election victory that gave him control of the Senate. Upon gaining the freedom to pass any legislation he wanted without needing to make compromises to win crossbench support, Howard's image quickly reverted to the ultra-conservative, out-of-touch one that had dogged him in the 1980s and early 1990s, and he reverted to being unelectable.

Howard's signature WorkChoices industrial relations reforms ultimately reduced his own options for continued employment, and he lost not only the prime ministership, but his own seat.

His defeat also came courtesy of a brilliant campaign by Kevin Rudd, who had realised that Australian voters above all else sought reassuring blandness from their leaders, and proceeded to deliver it in abundance. Rudd also managed to conceal his true personality from the electorate until the first words of his victory speech.*

Early life

John Howard was raised in Earlwood, inspiring his lifelong love of the monarchy. Conventionally for a Liberal leader, he graduated from law at the University of Sydney; but unconventionally, he attended a public school—Canterbury Boys' High School. This was, of course, long before it became one of the most multicultural schools in the state.

Political career

Howard joined the Liberal Party in 1957, and, as a self-described con-servative, dedicated his subsequent five decades in public life to keeping Australia in that same year.

He was elected to federal parliament in 1974, and held his seat of Bennelong—fittingly named after the first Aboriginal man to travel to Britain and attempt to integrate with Europeans—for the next 33 years.

---

* Which were 'Okay guys', rebranding Rudd immediately as a school principal who thinks he's 'hip to the kids'.

Malcolm Fraser appointed him as treasurer in 1977, and Howard was Australia's first economic custodian to support free-market economics. This made him unpopular with his more protectionist leader, especially when Howard publicly endorsed Bob Hawke's election in 1983, on the basis that voters had chosen with their suddenly visible hand.

Howard contested the vacant leadership of the party, but was defeated by Andrew Peacock—the two men would battle until 1990 for the right to keep the Liberals unelectable.

One Australia

Howard's signature One Australia policy, released in 1988, called for an end to multiculturalism. To support it, he famously suggested that Asian immigration should 'be slowed down a little'. Though history has been damning of this position, achieving it would have benefited him personally—Asian migrants played a large part in the then-PM losing his seat in 2007, suggesting his limited understanding of the Asian notion of karma.

As part of 'One Australia', Howard opposed a treaty with Aboriginal people and promoted a common Australian culture. It should be noted, however, that the One Australia policy cannot be considered the forerunner of Pauline Hanson's One Nation, except in terms of its similar name, its similar resistance to immigration and multiculturalism, its similar belief that Aboriginal people should not get special treatment, and its similar insistence there is one unique Australian identity to which all should subscribe.

One Australia's most immediate effect, however, was to safeguard one Australia under Labor rule—leading to the implementation of Keating's One Nation policy, which had an identical name to Hanson's party but an opposite goal. It's believed that Hanson would never have used the same name as Keating had she been paying any attention whatsoever to national affairs.

Return to leadership

Following equally unsuccessful periods under Andrew Peacock (again), John Hewson and Alexander Downer, Howard found himself leader of the opposition once more. He had once described his chances as being equivalent to those of Lazarus with a triple bypass—in fact, they were equivalent to Steve Bradbury with a triple collision.

Paul Keating had pulled off one impossible election victory in 1993 despite his widespread unpopularity; a second was beyond him, and so John Howard became prime minister at last, partly by virtue of his extraordinary persistence, and mostly by default.

Prime minister (1996–2007)

First term

Having inflicted a huge defeat on the Keating government, Howard arrived in Canberra as the oldest of new brooms.

His first major challenge was the Port Arthur massacre, in response to which he passed sweeping gun reforms, which have been so successful that there have been no mass shootings in the more than 20 years since. Despite an intense backlash that led to him appearing in front of a pro-gun crowd in a bulletproof vest, Howard prevailed, and significantly enhanced his standing with the electorate due to his bravery in passing a bold social reform. After this stunning initial success, the new prime minister would never again attempt to depart from traditional conservative values.

Howard instead boldly opposed native title rights for Aboriginal people after *Wik*; union rights on the waterfront; and the influence of Pauline Hanson, by rushing to condemn her controversial maiden speech a mere seven months after it was delivered. He ultimately neutralised One Nation as a political force by adopting much of its hardline stance.*

Perhaps Howard's bravest move during his first term, however, was his decision to take a goods and services tax (GST) to the election. Some polls had been unfavourable, and Howard decided that he would go down fighting for the thing he believed in most fervently of all—regressive tax reform.

In the October 1998 election, the Australian people chose to dump Howard's Coalition government after just one term, and Kim Beazley's victory in the popular vote was an extraordinary result, given the extent of Labor's losses less than three years earlier.

However, due to a minor technicality concerning the geographical distribution of Labor's majority vote, Howard was in fact re-elected with a 12-seat majority.

Second term

Early in his second term, Howard delivered on his promise to recognise popular support for an Australian republic, by holding a constitutional convention to determine the model that would be put to the Australian people.

---

* Arguably by clawing back the platform that he had pioneered himself.

The PM was torn between his strict opposition to any change and his fondness for convention.

Even though most Australians supported a republic, Howard had learned in 1998 that losing the majority doesn't mean losing the contest, and so the argument over the model ultimately derailed the 'yes' vote, leading to the defeat of the referendum. Howard knew from his time in student politics that the left would much rather wait for

THE PRIME MINISTER
OF AUSTRALIA

Howard pictured behind a sign confirming he was PM, just in case people didn't believe it.

perfection than vote for an imperfect compromise, and consequently the republicans are still waiting for their chance to vote for the 'superior' direct election model nearly 20 years later.

Howard's second term was dominated by the implementation of the GST—by passing it, he expunged not only a raft of complex, archaic taxes but also the Australian Democrats.

Australian troops were also deployed as peacekeepers to keep East Timor safe, a gesture that was somewhat undermined by the attempt to also keep most of Timor's oil safe in Australian hands. This principle had previously been established via the Timor Gap Treaty with Indonesia—the name refers to the gulf between what Australia morally deserved and what it ultimately took.

During this period, Howard came under sustained pressure to apologise to the Stolen Generations—displaying his trademark stubbornness, he not only never apologised, but since leaving office, has never apologised for not apologising.*

Howard's second term looked like ending in defeat, but the twin threats of 9/11 and the prospect of 433 rescued asylum seekers being allowed to disembark from the *Tampa* onto Australian soil changed public opinion. The electorate voted on the basis of security, and chose to protect the nation from Kim Beazley.

Third term

2001–4 were dominated by Australia's involvement in the wars in Afghanistan and Iraq, linked by the Bush administration as the 'war on terror', although not in any other sense. Howard famously said of the invasion 'it is right, it is lawful, and it is in Australia's national interest', a statement in which the only accurate words were 'it is'.

Australia's involvement in the 'coalition of the oiling' helped to give America the figleaf of international endorsement for a military campaign that was unrelated to the 9/11 attack, but made Americans feel powerful again, despite their ongoing failure to capture Osama bin Laden.

Nevertheless, Howard's agreement to involve Australia was skilfully negotiated so that troop casualties were minimised, an admirable result. It was unfortunate that the more than 100,000 Iraqis who died during the conflict did not have Mr Howard to negotiate for them.

Back home, Howard made an error that's been nicknamed 'the Downer' by political scientists—the political mistake of being too effective against

---

* Instead, Kevin Rudd apologised in a moment of potent symbolism for the nation. It was the one moment where his preference for words over actions delivered a significant result.

a weak opponent, leading to their replacement by somebody who's more of a threat. The Labor leader, Simon Crean, failed to make an impact against Howard despite the growing unpopularity of the Iraq war. As a result, Crean was replaced by Mark Latham, who soon led Howard in the polls.

Eventually, Latham's support collapsed, after an awkward photo of the two leaders shaking hands made it appear as though the Labor leader were trying to physically intimidate Howard—in other words, a standard Latham greeting.

Ultimately, the electorate turned on the challenger and gave Howard a fourth term. His success in saving Australia from having Mark Latham as prime minister is now seen as his greatest national security accomplishment, especially by Labor voters.

Fourth term

As Howard celebrated ten years in office in 2006, it was revealed that he had promised Peter Costello he would retire after approximately five years in office. Many called for the treasurer to either quit his portfolio or challenge his boss—but Costello, with a characteristic display of fortitude, chose neither.

Instead of retiring unchallenged on his tenth anniversary, Howard held on for the 2007 APEC conference in Sydney, which achieved little besides amusement at President Bush calling it 'OPEC'. Ultimately, Howard resolved the leadership issue by promising to stand down for Costello if he won a fifth term. Thanks to the treasurer's level of popularity, this vow ultimately became yet another reason not to re-elect the Coalition.

Kim Beazley had returned as Labor leader after the despondent party had sought someone more competent than Crean and less unstable than Latham. But yet another run of poor personal polling led him to be replaced by Kevin Rudd in December 2006. Promising a fresh yet non-radical face, Rudd's ability to project sunny, youthful dullness finally proved Howard's nemesis.

Legacy

In terms of his duration in office, if not his achievements, Howard is ranked behind only his hero, Sir Robert Menzies, a man who inspired his successor's famous rejection of the 'black armband view of history'— Howard having reasoned that Australia's post-1788 history could not be considered problematic when so much of it was shaped by Menzies.

Howard's own dubious nostalgia for the halcyon days of Menzies is now matched by an equally fervent nostalgia by his parliamentary successors for his own era in office, when tough decisions like the GST could be made, the polls would be disastrous as a result, and then a *Tampa* or a Mark Latham would sail into view just in time to win the government another term.

John Howard's four election victories and 11 years in office rewrote the rules of Australian politics, and his political legacy is that leaders on both sides of the aisle now doggedly refuse to retire even after the most devastating of failures.*

Howard proved that no matter how unlikely it may seem that a failed leader will be resurrected, it's a safe bet that their replacements will at

---

* See entry **Tony Abbott**.

some point falter even more catastrophically, leading to a known quantity seeming like a steady hand. This is why, though he has now been in retirement for a decade, a fifth Howard term cannot be ruled out.

Iced VoVo

The **Iced VoVo** is a uniquely Australian biscuit, in that it was designed by a committee, resulting in a series of compromises that fail to satisfy anybody. It is in many respects the biscuit equivalent of Australia's parliament, which combines a British-style lower house with an American-style upper house, combining the worst elements of both systems.

Recipe

An Iced VoVo is a hybridised compromise between several different styles of unhealthy biscuits. First, it's iced with hard, generic fondant, forming a sugary crust whose flavour is best described as 'pink'. Then, a stripe of raspberry jam is added, similarly hardened so it cannot smear easily. Finally, a dandruff of coconut is sprinkled on top, making it somewhat, but ultimately not enough, like a lamington.

History

Iced VoVos have been eaten by Australians since 1906, when they ranked just below dripping and sheep's head soup as a popular delicacy. Since those days, the iconic snack lost favour as the public discovered every other variety of biscuit. Nevertheless, it's produced to this day by Arnott's, the best-known Australian biscuit manufacturer that's under American ownership. Australians still enjoy an Iced VoVo, especially with tea, because if you dip them in tea, they taste more like tea.

In his victory speech after being elected prime minister in 2007, Kevin Rudd joked that his team could have a strong cup of tea and an Iced VoVo before getting to work. Political scientists have calculated that this was the precise moment when many Australians began to regret electing him prime minister.

Ned Kelly

Edward 'Ned' Kelly (December 1854–11 November* 1880) was a folk hero, legend, icon and the symbol of a nation.

It's also been alleged by the state, and associated organs of bland conformity, that he happened to be a bushranger who murdered several police officers, but in a land with an extensive convict heritage that's short on popular heroes, it's been agreed by the majority of Australians that this shouldn't diminish his iconic status in any way.

Early life

Ned Kelly's father, Red, was a freedom fighter from Ireland, who had been transported to Van Diemen's Land for freeing pigs. Upon release, he moved to Beveridge, Victoria, and began freeing cattle into a special kind of liberty where Kelly could do with them as he wished. He built a house that soon became notorious as a rendezvous for fellow freedom

---

* Australia's traditional day to remove anti-establishment figures.

advocates wanting to keep a low profile by hanging out with a convicted criminal.

The Kellys subsequently moved to Avenel, where Red was soon convicted for having liberated a bullock hide. He died shortly after his own liberation from the resulting imprisonment, leaving a strong impression on young Ned, who soon began gifting freedom to local cattle and horses as well.

Ned's first brush with the law came at the age of 14, when Ned kindly helped Ah Fook, a passing trader, lighten his heavy load by 10 shillings. Kelly ended up taking to the bush with his associates, while his mother was convicted.

Eventually, Ned and his men liberated several police constables from the heavy burden of having to track and capture the Kelly gang, and freed them from the shame of having to live with the knowledge that they had arrested Australia's greatest folk hero. It was for this crime of mercy killing that Ned Kelly was ultimately martyred.

Following this incident, the Victorian government paid Ned Kelly and his brother Dan the compliment of securing their legend by declaring them outlaws. This meant they could be shot on sight, and that anybody could be punished for helping them, which had the effect of instantly making the Kellys the most popular men in Victoria.

Ned Kelly and his men continued to rampage across the state's rural areas, helping foster local development in a way that government never could, by robbing banks and spreading the money through the community. They also promoted community harmony, considerately relieving an unpopular police informant of his life.

The Kelly gang made their final stand in Glenrowan. The rest of Ned's associates obligingly died during the stand-off, allowing their leader to become the sole focus of the subsequent trial, and subsequently a legend. The hero was captured despite wearing body armour after police cheated by shooting him in the legs.

After a trumped-up trial in which Kelly was wrongly convicted on the basis of the things he had done, he was sentenced to death, and with it, immortality.

He was survived by his voluminous beard and an even more voluminous legend. Ever a selfless man, despite his lifelong practice of

It's believed that Ned Kelly would have been able to escape the troopers had he not been weighed down by that beard.

taking other people's property for his own personal use, his adventures have gifted the otherwise unremarkable town of Glenrowan a thriving tourist industry to this very day.

Legacy

Ned Kelly is undoubtedly Australia's most popular outlaw hero—admittedly, not a great accomplishment when its second-most prominent celebrity felon is Rolf Harris.

Kelly attempted to justify his actions by criticising the police and blaming them for their harsh sectarian treatment of Irish Catholics. The detailed, insulting description of police in his famous Jerilderie letter is enough to win over anybody who's ever resented the pompous officer who pulled them over for a breath test. Not being trained in the finer points of rhetoric, however, Kelly does his case a considerable disservice by confessing to most of the crimes of which he'd been accused.

Kelly's trademark metal helmet appears in dozens of artworks by Sidney Nolan. It's believed that Nolan favoured the Kelly image not just for its potent symbolism, but because it was quicker to finish when he didn't have to paint a face.

The outlaw is the subject of Yahoo Serious's second movie, *Reckless Kelly*, which raised an interesting philosophical conundrum—if a film is released and only a handful of people watch it, can it truly be said to have been released at all?

It's been widely misreported that Ned Kelly's last words were 'Such is life'. Though this was a favourite expression, his last words were, in fact, 'Please don't let Mick Jagger play me in a film.'

Nicole Kidman

'Our' Nicole Kidman is an Australian–American Oscar-winning actress. Her best-known role, however, is as Tom Cruise's second wife, one for which she was plucked from obscurity and transported straight to the red carpets of Hollywood. The marriage did not survive and, in fact, her suffering began even before they established a romantic relationship, when she found herself starring opposite him in a Jerry Bruckheimer movie, *Days of Thunder*.

Although Kidman's acting career has been highly successful, critics agree that she was a total failure as a Scientologist.

Nowadays, Kidman is married to the country music star Keith Urban, with whom she has a great deal in common, including being largely absent from Australia, and succeeding overseas despite widespread bemusement and scepticism back home.

Kidman specialises in playing experts, inspired by her psychologist father to play neurosurgeons, translators, nuclear physicists and the like, and playing women trapped in oppressive marriages inspired by another man who was once in her life. She has occasionally tried to appear in comedies (*Bewitched*), and has occasionally appeared in unintentional ones (*Batman Forever*)—Kidman now steers clear of humour and, indeed, smiling in general.

The actress has confessed to using Botox but, while using it, still managed to produce moving performances, even if her face wasn't at the time. She now claims to be free of the treatment, but if she isn't and was joking, there would be no way of telling from her expression.

Kidman is unquestionably one of Australia's most successful leading ladies, even though she wasn't *Australia*'s successful leading lady.

Prominent film roles

BMX Bandits (1983)—the teenaged Kidman prodigiously inhabits the role of Judy, a freckly Australian girl from Sydney's Northern Beaches who likes riding bikes. A towering performance that was inexplicably snubbed by the Academy.

One BMX Bandit went on to steal Australia's heart.

Dead Calm (1989)—the role in which Tom Cruise noticed her, this thriller sees Kidman trapped on a boat with a terrifyingly unhinged man. It inspired Cruise to leave her trapped in a mansion with a terrifyingly unhinged man.

Days of Thunder (1990)—Kidman plays a brain surgeon, plausibly, who falls for Cruise's NASCAR driver, implausibly.

Far and Away (1992)—Kidman plays an Irish lass who falls in love with an American attempting to disguise himself as an Irishman, played by Tom Cruise. Though he regularly lapses into his American accent, Kidman's character politely pretends she can't tell.

To Die For (1995)—Kidman plays a deeply unpleasant person who will do anything for fame and publicity. Critics have commented that she 'really inhabited the role'.

Batman Forever (1995)—Kidman plays Batman's psychologist love interest, Dr Chase Meridian, as well as can be expected, which is, given the script, not well at all. The only positive thing that can be said about this film is that unlike its successor, *Batman and Robin*, it doesn't have Arnold Schwarzenegger as Mr Freeze saying 'Let's kick some ice'.

Eyes Wide Shut (1999)—Kidman's last performance opposite Tom Cruise, the film revolves around a couple with a weird relationship who struggle with the line between fantasy and reality. It's not clear where Stanley Kubrick got the idea, but there are theories.

Moulin Rouge! (2001)—Kidman plays a courtesan, Satine, in a hyper-real Baz Luhrmann pop culture pastiche. Her singing led to a fresh appreciation of her acting talent.

The Hours (2002)—Kidman won the Best Actress Oscar for playing Virginia Woolf, and particularly for her bravery in donning a prosthetic nose to do so. It was this acclaimed performance that gave her the misconception that having parts of her face that didn't move would make her a more successful actress.

The Stepford Wives (2004)—Kidman plays against type by being the one non-robotic woman in town.

The Golden Compass (2007)—Kidman plays a terrifying ice queen who wants to split children from their souls. It's been hailed as one of her most likeable performances.

Australia (2008)—let's just say it happened, and she was in it.

Rabbit Hole (2010)—Kidman was nominated for a Best Actress Oscar for her role as a bereaved mother who falls apart. However, as it grossed only a couple of million, the film was mostly bereaved of an audience.

Grace of Monaco (2014)—Kidman plays a Hollywood actress who finds herself in an unexpectedly difficult marriage with someone incredibly famous. Even so, many critics found her performance unconvincing.

Lion (2016)—Kidman plays an ordinary suburban Australian woman with a dodgy perm who adopts two kids. She was nominated for a Best Supporting Actress Oscar for this performance, which some have suggested she was preparing for her entire life.

Koala

The **koala** (*Phascolarctos lazyarsus*) is a marsupial that is one of the most indolent creatures on the planet, yet, curiously, also one of the most likely to contract a sexually transmitted disease.

The koala's cute, sleepy demeanour conceals a rapacious sexual appetite. *Summi*

They are often assumed to be bears[*] but, in fact, their closest relative is the wombat, which is to say that they're pretty much out on their own.

Humans are extremely fond of koalas, perhaps because we increasingly share their pudgy appearance, and have a similar approach to our diet, as both humans and koalas tend to consume food that is both low in nutrients and highly toxic, greatly restricting our physical movement as a result.

Male koalas also particularly resemble their Australian human counterparts, in that they mature sexually later than women, and spend much of their lives bellowing and brawling.

In recent years, koalas have become widely affected by chlamydia and koala immune deficiency syndrome,[†] or KIDS, which is similar to AIDS. This is thought to be because the lack of energy caused by their paltry eucalyptus-leaf diet has left them too exhausted to go and buy condoms.

Koalas also generally can't be bothered outrunning bushfires, while male koalas are incapable of determining when female koalas are in heat, despite the clear physical signs. Most naturalists concede that it's astonishing that they've survived until now.

---

[*] Mostly by Americans.

[†] This is real. And really known as KIDS.

Nevertheless, what with being perpetually intoxicated and ridden with sexually transmitted diseases, koalas have done all that they possibly could to shake off their cutesy image. Unfortunately, nobody has paid much attention, so it's all been to no avail for this Macaulay Culkin of the marsupial kingdom.

Lagerphone

The **lagerphone** is a musical instrument that produces sound by being shaken, hammered into the ground and laughed at. It's the most Australian of instruments, as it is associated with both beer and a criminal who was incarcerated on the other side of the world.

To construct a lagerphone, one must first consume a large quantity of beer. This is so that one will have enough bottle tops to build it, and also so that one will think that making a lagerphone is a good idea.

The explosion of craft beer in recent years has also led hipsters to construct craft lagerphones, which are generally used to construct arty, abstract soundtracks to the conceptual short films that their owners are totally going to make some day.

The town of Brooweena in Queensland claimed in 2009 to have set an unofficial record for the most people simultaneously playing the lagerphone: 134. Why they chose to do this has not been recorded, but most likely involved the consumption of 1340 bottles of beer.

Lake George

Lake George is a lake in south-eastern New South Wales, except when it isn't. It's found, or not found, roughly 40 kilometres north-east of Canberra, along the Federal Highway, to which it provides either charming water views or dull lake-bed views.

The lake is either 25 or 0 kilometres long and 10 or 0 kilometres wide. It's extremely shallow, with a very small catchment, and is an endorheic lake, meaning that it is not connected with the outside world in any way. This is perhaps why Lake George has become such an enduring symbol of Canberra.

It was named for King George III, who was known for his highly erratic behaviour, making him the obvious namesake for this particular lake/bare patch of dusty soil. Equally fittingly, the lake's Aboriginal name, Werriwa, was given to the seat once held by Mark Latham.

The Capital Wind Farm, NSW's largest, is located on the edge of the lake. It's either a hideous eyesore or an exciting renewable energy project, depending on your politics.

It's possible to both fish and graze sheep in the middle of Lake George, but it's advisable to check the water level first.

Mark Latham

Mark 'The Outsider from *Outsiders*' Latham is a former politician, former left-winger, and formerly respected public intellectual. A Gough Whitlam protégé who was once considered to be destined for greatness, he led the Australian Labor Party to one of its greatest-ever losses, at the 2004 federal election.

Although it's been easy to forget in recent years, Latham was once elected by members of the Labor Party—not the Liberal Party—to lead the federal parliamentary *Labor* party. This was because he was seen to represent a clean break after Kim Beazley and Simon Crean. He still does, although in a rather different manner, as those two men are still beloved as Labor elders. Latham's most famous clean break, however, was of a taxi driver's arm.*

Always a combative figure, Latham famously referred to the Coalition frontbench as a 'conga line of suckholes', providing one of the most memorable post-Keating insults in Australian politics. He would go on in his post-parliamentary life to latch onto the rear of this conga line, and particularly former minister Ross Cameron. Eventually, Latham's politics gravitated to the right of most of the Liberal Party.

Once considered Labor's most prominent intellectual and reformer, he wrote the influential book *Civilising Global Capital* before going on to prove that civility was not, in fact, within his arsenal of talents.

He had a column with the *Australian Financial Review* before he was sacked, appeared regularly on Channel Nine's *The Verdict* before it was axed, and appeared on Sky News' *Outsiders* before he was fired. He is now as much of an outsider as you can be while living on a generous parliamentary pension—the same parliamentary pension he was instrumental in removing for those parliamentarians who came after him.

---

* In hindsight, this should have been an entirely clear warning sign.

Latham famously had a testicle removed after a broadcast on the ABC led him to check himself, although his regard for the national broadcaster has now gone the same way as the organ in question. Latham has been hailed as conclusive medical proof that losing a testicle need not impede a worrying excess of testosterone.*

At the time of writing, Latham has begun broadcasting live via social media. Given his commentary career to date, he seems likely to be the first person ever to be sacked from his own Facebook page.

Literature in Australia

Australian literature is written or literary work produced in the Commonwealth of Australia, an explanation which is as unnecessary as many of its examples. Most Australian literature deals with the compelling majesty of the landscape, the country's problematic race relations, and, in one of its most popular series, a brilliant renegade Marine who has to wear sunglasses because of the vertical scars on his eyes.

Prominent Australian writers

Peter Carey—a dual Booker winner, who for some inexplicable reason mainly writes about Australia, despite having lived for many years in New York. Widely considered to be our top contender for the Nobel Prize in Literature, along with Iggy Azalea.

JM Coetzee—unquestionably Australia's greatest South African novelist.

---

* Or its sometime by-product, rage.

Helen Demidenko/Darville—her novel *The Hand that Signed the Paper* briefly got everyone talking about Australian fiction again, but only because it was masquerading as non-fiction.

C.J. Dennis—famous for his verse novel *The Songs of a Sentimental Bloke*, which is the last time that any Australian male confessed to any sentiment whatsoever.

Nick Earls—came to prominence with semi-autobiographical novels about socially awkward young men who were inexplicably attractive to various gorgeous women. Earls is intriguingly reticent about exactly how autobiographical they are.

Bob Ellis—as well as being a gifted screenwriter and speechwriter, Ellis's popular works of contemporary political history were adored by both the Labor true believers whose tales he told and the Liberal politicians who earned a motza from defamation payouts.

Richard Flanagan—unquestionably one of our greatest living novelists and finest storytellers, which makes it all the more surprising to learn that he worked on *Australia*.

Miles Franklin—primarily famous for a pioneering novel of female empowerment published under her middle name to disguise her female identity. Franklin is the namesake of two awards, the second of which, the Stella Prize, was founded as a reaction to the Miles Franklin being male-dominated—assuming that none of the finalists had also adopted a male-sounding pen name for the same reason Franklin did.

Helen Garner—an equally acclaimed writer of powerful fiction and thought-provoking non-fiction, including several acclaimed works that probe the moral complexities of tragic situations, Garner is probably Australia's least likely writer to produce a comic novel.

Germaine Greer—the iconic author of *The Female Eunuch*, Greer's era-defining, globally significant work as a pioneer of second-wave feminism is undermined a little more with every appearance on *Q&A*.

Kate Grenville—writer of several extraordinary novels about race relations in early New South Wales, based on her own family history, Grenville's powerful insights regrettably came several generations too late.

Thomas Keneally—one of Australia's best-loved novelists and popular historians, Keneally's fabled career shows young Australians eager to tell the engrossing stories of their homeland that the best path to international literary superstardom is to write a book about Nazis.

Dominic Knight—will never be invited to another writers' festival after publishing this list.*

David Malouf—one of the leading writers to come out of Queensland, and, in his case, never really to go back.

Sally Morgan—well known as the author of *My Place*, about her search for identity and knowledge of her family's past. Critics have accused the book of facilitating whitesplaining by Europeans who read it and then presume they understand and can speak about the Aboriginal experience at the hands of their ancestors, which Morgan says wasn't quite what she was aiming for.

Les Murray—not the legendary SBS football presenter, this Les Murray is known for his many highly acclaimed poetry collections, often revolving around his family's property at Bunyah. He's also known for wasting his time on John Howard's constitutional preamble.

Matthew Reilly—writes thrillers. Lots of thrillers. Full of action. Tough guys. Explosions. And very. Short. Sentences.†

Henry Handel Richardson—one of Australia's most acclaimed female writers of last century. Sad, isn't it?

---

* Also, this list is titled 'prominent'.

† You might think that this entry was inspired by jealousy of his sales. You would be right.

Christina Stead—writer of *The Man Who Loved Children*, a great Australian novel that her publisher forced her to rewrite so the Australians were Americans, and was then hailed as hugely insightful into the contemporary American family.

Christos Tsiolkas—after first developing an indie reputation writing edgy novels about young gay men, Tsiolkas's career took a dramatic leap forward after he started writing about parents of toddlers in the suburbs instead.

Patrick White—probably the most significant writer in the modern history of Australian literature, and our only winner of the Nobel Prize for Literature, which makes readers feel all the more guilty when they're unable to finish one of his novels.

David Williamson—the closest thing we have to a national playwright, he obtained highly positive critical attention with early plays that brilliantly deconstructed contemporary mores, and then slowly lost it with late plays railing against political correctness.

Tim Winton—has won many awards for repeatedly bringing drama, intrigue, romance and profundity to a place where many thought such a thing impossible: Western Australia.

Logie Awards

The **Logie Awards**, or **Australian television's night of nights**, are Australia's annual TV awards, presenting statuettes to the country's most popular programs, along with a few better-quality ones that nobody watched. The broadcasts of the awards used to be shared equally around all the networks, and is now shared equally around Channel Nine cost centres.

Created by *TV Week* magazine, the awards have long been invested with all the credibility and gravitas one would associate with a publication whose primary function is reporting soapie plot twists as though they were happening to real people.

Graham Kennedy, the 'King of Australian television', gave the awards their name, which derives from the middle name of an early pioneer of the medium, John Logie Baird. It became the comedy legend's most enduring joke, played on millions of television viewers for decades. Most insiders agree that it's now too late for the industry to change the name to something that wasn't suggested in jest.

The ceremony has taken place in the ballroom of Melbourne's Crown Casino for the past couple of decades, because Crown is Australia's largest venue purpose-designed for its patrons losing. In recent years, the winners have been required to stake their statuettes on the roulette table after coming off stage, which has led to considerable savings in the production budget. It has recently been announced that the Logies will move to a place as devoid of irony as the awards themselves—the Gold Coast.

Memorable Logies ceremonies include that time Andrew Denton hosted, the year where Steve Irwin's snake bit Tim Webster, and that other time Denton hosted.

There are many important Logies traditions, including awards being presented by minor international celebrities who don't bother to veil their contempt; guests perpetually leaving their tables so they can drink and gossip in the foyer without having to watch the ceremony; and attendees going on to present breakfast television the following morning while obviously intoxicated.

Unlike the Oscars, Logies are not awarded by the members of a broader Academy, but are either judged by a small panel or awarded via popular vote. *TV Week* has defended its process on the basis that anyone who wants to set up their own television awards can jolly well just go and do so.

In recent years, the competing AACTAs have been launched, in an attempt to create more reputable, industry-based awards, but the public has yet to fully embrace them because their name is highly confusing, as illustrated by the phrase 'Best Actor AACTA'.

The world's least precious gold item. *WikiCats*

The Logies are frequently criticised for being too long, too dull and largely irrelevant, but nobody can dispute that they would be the most fascinating show on television if the producers would only set up their cameras at the afterparties.

Key categories

Gold Logie—awarded to the most popular personality on Australian television. This used to be determined by the readers of *TV Week*, but they've now found an even more insubstantial method of casting votes: the internet.

Silver Logie for Best New Talent—for some briefly buzzy soap star who will never be heard of again.

Silver Logie for Most Popular Presenter—whoever most recently joined *The Project*.

Best Sports Program—the *NRL Footy Show* or, sometimes, for variation, the *AFL Footy Show*.

Best Lifestyle Program—something that allows viewers to fill their sorry lives with images of television personalities enjoying much better lives.

Best Reality Program—program from which any semblance of reality has been most skilfully removed.

Most Outstanding News Coverage—most heart-rending coverage of a natural disaster.

Most Outstanding Public Affairs Report—something that nobody watched, but everybody thought they should have.

Most Outstanding Comedy Program—something on the ABC.

Most Outstanding Factual Program—as this award was recently won by *Gogglebox Australia*, it's entirely unclear what this category is for.

Notable Gold Logie winners

Graham Kennedy (1960, 1967, 1969, 1974, 1978)—the greatest performer in the history of Australian television, he arguably should have won the Gold Logie every year, including posthumously.

Neil Armstrong and Buzz Aldrin (1970)—among the many accolades for their extraordinary achievement in becoming the first humans to walk on the moon, this honorary Gold Logie ranks as the most insignificant.

Norman Gunston (1976)—the first and only fictional character to win the Gold Logie, Gunston's nomination shouldn't even be possible, and yet here we are. In recent years, however, there has been a movement to nominate another imaginary TV presenter, Andrew Bolt.

Bert Newton (1979, 1981, 1982, 1984)—indelibly associated with the Logies, having hosted more of them than anybody else, Newton has nevertheless had a long and successful career in television.

Daryl Somers (1983, 1986, 1989)—though he won three times, it seems in hindsight more fitting to focus on the many dozens of years where he lost.

Ray Martin (1987, 1993–96)—'Australia's friend' ranks alongside Graham Kennedy as one of only two five-time winners. This surprises most viewers, who, given the parlous state of Australian television over many decades, assume it's even more.

Lisa McCune (1997–2000)—won for four straight years for *Blue Heelers*, highlighting the immense flaws of a system predicated on buying *TV Week*.

Rove McManus (2003–05)—won three years in a row because what the? His victories began a string of surprise Gold Logie wins for Channel Ten, which now regularly has more Logies voters than viewers.

Ray Meagher (2010)—won because the idea of voting for Alf from *Home and Away* is flaming hilarious until it happens and isn't.

Hamish Blake (2012)—won as part of an ongoing prank, and a broader professional tension, where he gets accolades and Andy doesn't.

Waleed Aly (2016)—made the kind of people who feel good about reading his columns and watching his 'nailed it' editorials on *The Project* feel good about his win, too. He is the first Muslim to win, which would be a powerful statement about diversity in Australia in an era of brewing intolerance were it not a Gold Logie.

Lollies

Lollies, or **sweets** if you're English, or **candy** if you absolutely must, are an integral part of the Australian diet. While in other countries, the excess consumption of lollies creates health problems such as obesity and diabetes, Australians are fortunate that the mild climate and natural beauty of their homeland make it easy to exercise away the intake of kilojoules and fats. Observing the svelte figure of the average Australian, one would never imagine that the consumption of chocolates, chips and sugary snacks is rampant.

For a small country that has long replicated popular brands from the UK and US, Australia has developed a surprisingly large number of its own iconic food brands for both the domestic market and export. This is because selling Australians unhealthy snacks is almost as reliably profitable as selling them beer.

Popular lollies

Fantales—toffees with wrappers displaying movie star biographies that would be perfect for guessing games with friends had the toffee not gummed your teeth together.

Redskins—Australia's most anachronistically racist snack product besides Coon cheese and Golliwog biscuits; the latter were renamed Scalliwags, in a move that did precisely nothing to solve the problem.

Wagon Wheel—round chocolate marshmallow biscuit, not to be used to repair an actual wagon.

Minties—lollies that taste like toothpaste and create an immediate need to use it.

Golden Rough—only the wrapper is golden, which is a bit rough.

Wizz Fizz—sherbet in a packet, not to be confused with its rock band form.

Chomp—aimed at young children, these chocolate bars helpfully contain usage instructions in the name.

Caramello Koalas—demonstrably less nutritious than actual koalas.

Freddos—an adorable smiling frog, whom you repay for his friendliness by devouring.

Tests have found this particular koala to be chlamydia-free. *Danarndt*

Killer Pythons—can kill even more slowly than actual pythons, via diabetes and heart failure.

Cadbury Top Deck—an uncomfortable metaphor for Australian race relations that places white pieces above layers of colour.

Fruit Tingles—for many years responsible for ruining Australian children's expectations of what fruit would taste like.

Wine Gums—their lack of alcoholic content has disappointed generations of teenagers.

Bertie Beetle—an unusual insect, whose exclusive habitat is the showbag pavilion.

Bullets—perfect if you want to be reminded of firearms every time you bite into a chocolate-covered mini liquorice.

Cadbury Snack—milk chocolate squares containing six different multicoloured syrups that vaguely reference established flavours. One of the enduring mysteries of Cadbury's business is who buys enough of Snack to keep it on sale.

Jaffas—chocolates covered in a sugary red shell, these were famously rolled down the aisles in cinemas, constituting a health hazard, but probably less of one than eating the whole packet.

Musk sticks—a staple of any lolly bag at a primary school birthday party, but rejected by everybody old enough to buy their own.

Freckles—those who grew up with freckles will appreciate the efforts of this product to make freckles a source of celebration rather than teasing, but, unfortunately, as they bear no resemblance to actual freckles, they're only of limited assistance.

Mad Max

Mad Max is universally recognised as the most accurate portrayal of Australia ever committed to the big screen. Its depiction of a world where car-obsessed weirdos drive vast distances across sparse landscapes, frequently confronting violent police who routinely exceed their authority, shows Australian outback life at its purest.

Mad Max's depiction of a desert world whose inhabitants would break any moral boundary in order to obtain oil has also predicted modern society, especially as such behaviour tends to result in brutal conflicts conducted in deserts.

For many years, *Mad Max* was the most profitable film relative to its budget of all time. So successful has the movie been that if you include its figures, the Australian film industry as a whole almost breaks even.

Mad Max, or as he'd be known today, YouTube Commenter Max.

Real-world parallels

Apart from its uncanny focus on the world's desertification and humans' increasing desperation for oil, the film and its title also predicted its star Mel Gibson's series of unhinged, rage-fuelled outbursts decades before they occurred. Like Max Rockatansky, Gibson would slip outside the bounds of normal society and then wander off, only to return a few years later because of the demands of the box office.

At its climax, Max sets his antagonist, Johnny, a choice between sawing off his foot or through a pair of handcuffs before he's blown up by a bomb on a timer, and then abandons him. This dilemma not only inspired the *Saw* series, but Australia's asylum seeker policy.

The series' director, George Miller, went on to helm an even more chilling portrayal of a post-apocalyptic nightmare world, *Happy Feet*.

Sequels

***Mad Max* 2 (1981)**—Max helps some desert settlers defend themselves against marauders who want to take their oil, foreshadowing the Iraq War from the Iraqi perspective.

***Mad Max Beyond Thunderdome* (1985)**—another successful sequel, it's now unwatchable due to the inclusion of Tina Turner's 'We Don't Need Another Hero'. 'Thunderdome' has become the generic term for any arena where there are regular, brutal fights to the death—in particular, the American political system, and *Married at First Sight*.

***Mad Max: Fury Road* (2015)**—the reboot won a spectacular reception after a lengthy break, despite the absence of the maddest member of the original team. *Mad Max: Fury Road* proved beyond doubt that highly profitable, critically acclaimed blockbusters could emerge from the Australian film industry as long as they were made by the only director who's ever known how to do it.

Meat pies

A **meat pie**, more accurately called a **'meat' pie**, is the national dish of Australia. The average Australian eats 12 meat pies per year, which helps explain why the average Australian is also significantly overweight.

In Australia, meat pies are ubiquitous wherever convenience foods are sold and no other form of hot food is available. They can be found at corner stores, milk bars, petrol stations, and especially at midwinter football games, where they are primarily used as handwarmers.

According to Australian food standards, a meat pie is required to have 25 per cent meat content meaning that they should more accurately be named 'Other stuff and meat pies'. Many pie manufacturers have been found to have fallen short of this very low bar. Under current regulations, buffalo, camel, deer, goat and hare are acceptable, a fact that, when discovered, generally prevents anyone from ever eating meat pies again.

Most Australian food writers believe that the meat pie's popularity results entirely from its usefulness as a handy edible platter for tomato sauce.

Melbourne

Melbourne is Australia's second largest city, and is widely tipped to overtake Sydney in population in the next few years, although not in global significance. Three-quarters of the state's population of 6 million live in the greater Melbourne area, and the next-largest city has a mere 140,000 residents, which is why there's a movement to rename the state 'Melbourne', on the basis that the rest is either outer suburbs or really, really outer suburbs.

It is the capital of Victoria, an enclave in the south-east corner of the mainland that considers itself the most cosmopolitan and European part of the nation, which is accurate in that it's small and cold. Victoria is one of Australia's two states named after the former Queen of England, out of a total of just six overall. The name also creates ambiguity with the Victorian era, especially since both it and the state contain a large quantity of men with waxed moustaches and jaunty peaked caps.

Melbourne is Australia's only city founded by a superhero, John Batman, who is known for setting up shop in dank, dark, cave-like places.

Like its namesake, Federation Square is a jumbled design devised in Melbourne.
Edwin.11

At the time of its settlement in 1835, Melbourne was part of New South Wales, which is important to remind its residents regularly. However, Victoria's settlers came from what was then known as Van Diemen's Land, making their ongoing refusal to give Tasmania an AFL team seem like the action of a brattish child.

Geography

The central business district of Melbourne consists of a grid that is aligned with the Yarra River. While at first it may seem small by the standards of most international cities, it's important to note that the residents favour tiny, tucked-away spaces. A decrepit basement with a low ceiling and a persistent smell of engine oil tucked beneath a drab carpark is considered a more valuable location for a hot new nightclub,* for instance, than a large, prominent building in a good location.

The south side of the river, imaginatively known as Southbank,† is an innovative social experiment designed to discover what would happen if a suburb were devoted exclusively to monolithic arts buildings, hotels, serviced apartments and a casino. Preliminary findings have been discouraging.

The city can easily be navigated by tram for those who like travelling at walking pace without moving their legs,‡ while Melbourne's extensive suburban train network occasionally thrills locals by working, and even arriving on time. Due to extensive privatisation, however, seeing staff at train stations is incredibly rare, and generally considered sufficient justification to call in news crews.

Non-locals are discouraged from driving in the CBD, as there is a strange manoeuvre known as the 'hook turn', which requires those turning right across tram tracks, for instance, to do so from the left on a red light. It generally proves fatal to any visitor.

Culture

Melbourne locals regularly claim that their city is Australia's cultural capital, as a way of consoling themselves because they don't have the Sydney Opera House.

---

* There are several in Melbourne's CBD, offering convenient parking for patrons in no condition to drive home.

† Brisbane's older South Bank, which is also the home to its ABC building and various cultural institutions, is spelled with a space, so it's not like Melbourne copied the idea.

‡ City trams are now free, which seems fair.

The city has a vibrant festival scene, which gives locals something to do on the weekend during the 11 months of the year when going to one of the city's drab beaches isn't a viable option. Among other subjects, Melbourne hosts festivals for comedy, film, music and smugness.

White Night is a particularly popular event. The city's cultural precinct stays open until dawn so that Melburnians can gather at various major venues to talk about how Sydney doesn't have White Night.

Melbourne is undeniably the fashion capital of the country for all who like their moustaches waxed and their greys muted, and enjoy wearing thick coats throughout the year.

The state's capital is known for its buzzing laneways, because there's something about the wide boulevards created by the city's original design-ers that makes you want to squeeze into the tiniest thoroughfare possible. Visitors to Melbourne are invariably surprised by the town planners' decision to put the most vibrant parts of the city in its narrowest spaces, but Melbourne has always been a city where exclusivity is prized, to the point where its bouncers will often turn visitors away from an empty bar, citing a 'private party'.

Melburnians love their sport, and their city is the home of Australian rules football, being the least tiny settlement where a critical mass of people care about it. There is also an extremely well attended Comedy Festival, started by Barry Humphries back before his major professional interest was railing against political correctness. However, visitors are advised to make themselves familiar with Melbourne's distinctive comedy customs, such as the most popular joke in any comic's set being directed at Frankston.*

---

* Making fun of Dandenong is also traditionally considered hilarious.

Architecture

Melbourne's urban architecture, seen in its iconic buildings like Federation Square and RMIT, is a unique style known as the 'mish mash'. It boldly mixes visual elements, any one of which would have been fine, but which clash violently when placed together.

Whereas contemporary architecture elsewhere is minimalist and uses glass extensively to make build-

Like Victoria's famous bushrangers, Crown Casino generally leaves members of the public with lighter pockets. *Edwin.11*

ings effectively disappear, much of Melbourne's recent architecture is designed to call attention to itself, culminating in the Eureka Tower, which is not only uncomfortably tall, but literally has a golden tip, making the nearby Crown Casino buildings look subtle by comparison. However, the upside of this style of architecture is that it draws visitors as rapidly as possible into the interior of the building, from where they can no longer see the outside.

Melburnians are known for irrepressible optimism about their city, best illustrated by their insistence that the north-east extremity of the city is its 'Paris end', an apt comparison for anyone who has never visited Paris.

Melbourne is, however, charmingly reminiscent of 1930s Chicago, on account of both its well-preserved Art Deco buildings and its regular outbursts of gangland violence.

Outer Melbourne

Geelong—the second-largest city in Victoria, meaning that it has an inferiority complex towards the city that has an inferiority complex towards Sydney.

Ballarat and Bendigo—both charming towns, which were once important centres of the Victorian gold rush and whose names start with 'B'. Nowadays, not even residents can remember the difference.

Warrnambool—despite popular misconception, this is not the home town of Victorian spin bowling legend Shane Warne.

Daylesford—a charming country town, where the best thing to do is have a cup of tea and browse antique shops. It's also the only thing to do.

Avalon—an example of how 'European' Victoria is, it's possible to board a flight to Melbourne and end up landing at this tin shed in the middle of nowhere, just like on Ryanair or easyJet. The only thing recommending Avalon Airport over Tullamarine is that it's closer to Geelong, which is not in fact a recommendation.

Melbourne's founder.

Bacchus Marsh—is the basis of Australian cricket's greatest nickname.

Glenrowan—scene of the last stand of the Kelly gang, some say that Ned surrendered, facing likely execution, just so he would be taken away from Glenrowan.*

---

* The definitive source of information on Glenrowan is *The Late Show*, which was on the ABC in the 1990s and broadcast a very funny and mean piece on the town. Search YouTube for 'Postcard from Glenrowan'.

Melbourne Cup

The **Melbourne Cup**, also known as **The Race That Stops The Nation** and **The Race That Should Be Stopped**, is an annual event designed for the efficient transfer of money from ordinary Australians to bookmakers, and horses from jockeys to dog-meat manufacturers.

A public holiday in Victoria and an excuse for workers to neglect their jobs across the rest of the country, the Melbourne Cup is held at Flemington on the first Tuesday in November each year. The day afterwards isn't technically a public holiday anywhere, but is treated as such by many employees, as the festivities generally leave them in no state to get out of bed.

The race is the culmination of Melbourne's Spring Racing Carnival, so called because, given Melbourne's climate, its residents wouldn't otherwise know that spring had arrived.

Format

The race is classed as a handicap for three-year-old and older horses, and for eighteen-year-old and older gambling addicts. It takes place over 3200 metres, or as many of them as horses can complete before breaking down and having to be put to 'sleep'.

The prize is currently $6.2 million, of which 85 per cent goes to the owner, 10 per cent goes to the trainer, 5 per cent goes to the jockey, and 0 per cent goes to the horse that did most of the work.

History

The idea for the Cup is credited to Frederick Standish, who had the notion of holding a horse race and calling it the Melbourne Cup, so people wouldn't make the natural assumption that, like any important event, it was held in Sydney.*

Its reputation as racing's premier demolition derby began with the first race, in 1861. One horse bolted, and three fell during the race, two of which died. Despite this, Melbourne thought it would be a jolly idea to continue the event.

Most distressingly of all for Melburnians, the first event was won by a Sydneysider. The horse, Archer, also won the second competition, and was prevented from competing in a third on some technicality because Melbourne.

Subsequently, the Cup's popularity grew quickly, probably because the tradition of awarding a public holiday to mark the occasion began as early as 1865.

The legendary Phar Lap competed three times, but only won once, in 1930, illustrating the utter futility of betting on a sport as unpredictable as horse racing.

In the past five years, four horses have died at, or in connection with, the Melbourne Cup. A much larger number of humans have died inside while gambling or drinking on Cup Day.

---

* Like every Sydneysider, the author of this book loves Melbourne, and wouldn't ever make fun of it if Melburnians didn't have such a massive chip on their shoulder about our city.

Off the track

'Fashions on the Field' is a popular feature of the day, partly because the Melbourne Cup only goes for three minutes out of the entire day, and also because being a clothes horse is relatively death-free.

Women often wear bizarre headpieces known as 'fascinators' to the Cup, for reasons involving irony. In 1965, model Jean Shrimpton made headlines around the world when she wore a miniskirt to the Cup, illustrating just how dull the world was in 1965.

Many celebrities attend the event and are fêted in various luxurious marquees, and the event ranks behind only the Logies as an occasion for celebrity misbehaviour. Gossip columnists are always free to concoct stories about fights that celebrities supposedly participated in during the race—as a rule, those named cannot remember a single thing about what they were doing that day, and therefore cannot sue.

Gambling on the Cup is, of course, the major purpose of the event. Many offices hold workplace sweeps, generally organised by the most junior member of the team, and entered into by the vast majority of workers on account of peer pressure and/or pity.

Sweeps also give to many Australians who would otherwise have no interest whatsoever in the Melbourne Cup a literal interest in it, if only that.

Famous winners

Malvolio (1891)—only winner to take out the trophy while cross-gartered and wearing yellow stockings.

Apologue (1907)—worst typo in Cup history.

The Trump (1937)—notable for its fake-looking ginger coat.

A horse surviving the Melbourne Cup is always a jubilant occasion. *Jupiter Firelyte*

Tawriffic (1989)—worst pun in Cup history, a more hotly contested field than the race itself.

Kingston Rule (1990)—fastest time, also first winner to be named after an Arnott's biscuit.

Subzero (1992)—its stablemates included Lemon Ruski and Vodka Cruiser.

Vintage Crop (1993)—first overseas horse to win the Cup, subsequently leading to annual protests about foreign horses coming and taking Australian jobs.

Ethereal (2001)—first horse to win while not physically present.

Makybe Diva (2003, 2004, 2005)—most wins and worst-spelled name.

Delta Blues (2006)—first Japanese horse to win the Cup, also first winner to subsequently become sashimi.*

---

* Known as basashi, per the Wikipedia article on 'horse meat'.

Midnight Oil

Midnight Oil, also known as **The Oils**, but soon to be renamed **Midnight Renewables**, are an iconic Australian rock band and interpretive dance troupe. Since 1972, the group has managed to simultaneously advocate activist hard-left values and amass substantial personal wealth.

Originally known as Farm, the band chose the name Midnight Oil with a draw from a hat, a difficult undertaking, as it was being used at the time to cover Peter Garrett's head. Although Garrett's vocals and dancing style are most politely described as unique, and his frequent departures to pursue other endeavours have placed the band on hold at various points, the other members of Midnight Oil will always be grateful for his arrival, as his singing technique made it impossible to continue as a Creedence Clearwater Revival cover band,* forcing them to write originals instead.

Midnight Oil are famous for their passionate live performances, and fans say that the intensity is only heightened by the real risk of those in the front few rows getting concussion from Garrett's flailing arms.

The Oils were formerly known for their combative attitude to the media, refusing to play the ABC's influential music program *Countdown* because of its requirement that artists mime to a recording—a policy that, hypo-critically, was never extended to the program's mumbling host.

Hiatus

Lead singer Peter Garrett has taken time out from the band on several occasions to pursue a political career. He unsuccessfully ran for the

---

* This is not a joke, but the idea of the Oils covering Creedence is pretty funny.

Senate with the Nuclear Disarmament Party in 1984, but his least successful involvement in politics followed his election as the Labor member for Kingsford Smith in 2004.

In 2007, new PM Kevin Rudd made him Minister for the Environment, which would have allowed him to pursue positive reforms in keeping with his lifelong green activism, had he not been part of the Rudd government.

Instead, he was lumped with administering a scheme to subsidise pink batt installations around the country. Introduced with great fanfare as part of Rudd's effort to overcome the global financial crisis, the haste and poor organisation of the campaign—which Garrett was later shown to have warned Rudd about on four occasions—had regrettable outcomes for to both his political career and a number of batt installers.

Garrett displayed the integrity and lack of killer instinct that made him so unsuitable to be a major-party politician by supporting Julia Gillard during the final, successful challenge from Kevin Rudd—he left politics at the 2013 election; arguably the best decision of his political career.

Reformation

Midnight Oil have reformed and have embarked on their 'Great Circle World Tour', named after the movements of Peter Garrett's arms. Though Garrett's career in Canberra was disappointing in most respects, it was hugely successful in increasing the demand for Midnight Oil concerts.

Milo

Milo is a chocolate malted-milk drink, that was first developed in Sydney in 1934. Around Australia, Milo is known for its sponsorship of junior cricket, which helps combat the juvenile obesity crisis brought on by consuming foods like chocolate malted-milk drinks. Its longtime slogan, 'You've gotta be made of Milo', is both untrue and scientifically impossible.

The inventor of Milo, Thomas Payne, tried for a long time to dissolve chocolate powder in milk, ultimately abandoning these efforts when his children said they enjoyed the crunch. Payne's invention has been recognised as one of Australia's most successful scientific failures ever.

Milo is marketed on the basis of its nutritional value, as the drink is fortified with vitamins and minerals that could otherwise only be obtained via a healthy, balanced diet. Nutritionists say that these additives can contribute to a nutritious diet if you ignore the sugar and fat you're consuming at the same time.

The drink is now popular around the world and, for decades now, this venerable 'dinky-di' brand has generated substantial revenues for that iconic Australian company, Nestlé. However, a recent co-branding program, designed to reach the growing alt-right community, ended in disaster and the widespread condemnation of 'Milo Yiannopoulos'.

Kylie Minogue

Kylie Ann Minogue, OBE, BUDGIE, best known simply as '**Kylie**', was born in the Melbourne suburb of Erinsborough on 17 April 1986.

Beginning her career as an overall-clad mechanic on *Neighbours*, Kylie's foray into music saw her continue this theme with songs entirely created by machines.

She released her first single, 'Locomotion', in 1987. A collaboration between Stock, Aitken, Waterman, a Casiotone synthesiser in demo mode and a broken fax machine, Kylie's original vocals were so heavily processed that she was unable to recognise herself in the final product, a result hailed by the production team as 'the point'. This first hit launched a thirty-year musical career and resulted in album sales of 80 million, and one good single.

Minogue's given name has proven an apt one for the star, as it means 'boomerang' in the Noongar language of Western Australia—that is, something that always makes a comeback.

Early career

Kylie has been based in London since the late 1980s, finding its weather 'like an even Melbournier Melbourne'. She nevertheless retains her girl-next-door appeal, if the girl next door had access to some of the world's top music producers.

Her more recent efforts, and singing lessons, have revealed Kylie as a genuinely accomplished singer, but this was not apparent in her early work. In her first iconic hit, 'I Should Be So Lucky', she sounded like her adenoids were blocked; in 'Hand on Your Heart', she sounded like she was singing beneath an ever-deepening layer of quicksand; in 'Je Ne Sais Pas Pourquoi', she sounded like her vocals had been overdubbed by Pepé Le Pew, and in 'Especially for You', she sounded like she'd been trapped in a recording studio with Jason Donovan.

She returned to acting with 1989's *The Delinquents*, in which Australia's sweetheart implausibly played a rebellious teen who was constantly in trouble with authority, and 1994's *Street Fighter*, in which she, even more implausibly, played a British Special Forces soldier. Her most true-to-life performance yet came in *San Andreas*, where she plays a woman who's overwhelmed by a digitally generated earthquake.

Current projects

Nowadays, Minogue is an internationally successful pop star, finally cracking the American market with her Grammy-winning album *Light Years*, a reference to the extremely long time it took her to make it there.

Kylie has also featured as a judge on several seasons of *The Voice*, where she had the audacity to critique singers' voices in the early phases of their careers.

Despite, or perhaps because of, her decades of enduring success, Kylie has proven unable to maintain a long-term relationship. But her sister, Dannii, nevertheless remains hopeful that her more successful big sis will one day return her calls.

National Broadband Network

The **National Broadband Network**, or **Notional Broadband Network** in much of the country, is a formerly ambitious program to connect Australian homes to the latest broadband technology.

Styled 'nbn' in the hope that a lower-case brand identity will lower expectations, it is now a program that's devoted to delivering very high internet speeds via a very slow rollout.

The NBN was initially dreamed up by the Rudd campaign in 2007 to emphasise its bold vision for the future, and after Rudd won the election, it instead emphasised his habit of forever talking about big ideas, while making glacially slow progress towards realising them.

Initially, the government planned to bypass Telstra's copper network entirely, connecting the majority via fibre to the home (FTTH). Under Julia Gillard, the fibre rollout began by connecting fibre in regional areas on the basis of need—specifically, the need to reward those crossbenchers who had supported her government.

When Labor lost in 2013, Malcolm Turnbull took charge of the NBN, partly on account of his portfolio as communications minister, but mostly because he was the only person in the new government who understood it. The incoming prime minister Tony Abbott also hoped that Turnbull's gift for verbosity would minimise one of the major policy areas where Labor had offered something better—this largely succeeded, as whenever Turnbull started talking about technical detail, the electorate's immediate impulse was to disconnect.

This enabled the Coalition to abandon the expensive FTTH model and instead adopt fibre to the node—the node being an ugly metal cabinet on street corners, from which Telstra's existing copper cable was used to connect to the house.

The advantage was that it was cheaper, although only in the short term; the disadvantage was that the speeds were slower and the entire point of the NBN had been to replace Telstra's decaying copper phone network.

This plan also meant that, shortly after selling off Telstra's ageing wiring at the peak of its value in a highly successful privatisation, the government now needed to ask for the old phone lines back at any price.

As the NBN's once-ambitious plans downscaled due to cost blowouts and the restrictions imposed by the Coalition, and the timetable dragged out even further, it gradually became clear

The NBN is bringing fast internet to our homes, and ugly boxes to everywhere else. *Bidgee*

that this supposedly futuristic broadband network would only arrive in most Australians' houses once mobile phone networks were capable of surpassing the NBN's current top speed of 100 megabits per second.

The NBN may never connect all Australia to a state-of-the-art broadband network, but its enduring value will most likely be as an illustration of why Australia hasn't done a terrific job of planning and delivering major infrastructure projects lately.

New Zealand

New Zealand (pronounced 'Nyoo Zullund' by locals) is an archipelago in the south-western Pacific Ocean to the south-east of the Australian mainland. While it sometimes maintains the pretence of not being part of Australia, there is freedom of movement and free trade between the areas, as well as a mutual defence treaty; its currencies are practically interchangeable; most of New Zealand's leading citizens relocate across the Tasman; and its flag is a tribute-band version of Australia's.

Consequently, the islands are for all intents and purposes part of the Commonwealth of Australia.

Relationship with Australia

Covering clause 6 of the Australian constitution lists the potential member states of the Commonwealth of Australia, including New Zealand. However, under Australia's federal system of government, New Zealand has been able to retain its parliament in Wellington and its legal system, including a relatively conciliatory approach to race relations that is unique within Australian states.

With approximately 4.8 million citizens, New Zealand's population is slightly smaller than Queensland's, making it the fourth-most-populous state in Australia. Nevertheless, it has almost double the population of Western Australia, ranked sixth. It's also closer to Sydney than Perth, both geographically and in terms of the frequency with which Sydneysiders remember it exists.

New Zealand has two main islands, the North-East Island or Te Ika-a-Māui, and the South-East Island, or Te Waipounamu. As part of the Pacific Ring of Fire, it's far more seismically active than the Australian mainland—the only respect in which there is more activity in New Zealand.

Taupo is one of the world's most active supervolcanoes, and the site of the most violent eruption anywhere in the world in the past 5000 years. Consequently, it's fortunate that New Zealand is considered part of Australia, in case its residents need to vacate suddenly.

Cultural connection with Australia

Despite its small size, New Zealand has contributed much to Australian cultural life. One of our most renowned actors, Russell Crowe, hails from Wellington; and Neil Finn, of our very own Crowded House, is based in Auckland. Some of the most creative parts of the Australian film industry are located in Wellington, while much of Flight of the Conchords' best material is about Australians.

Australia's own Neil Finn.
Mike Walen

One area where New Zealand is yet to achieve complete union with the rest of Australia is in sport. While its teams compete in most domestic competitions, it retains its own 'national' teams, rather like the friendly competition between England, Scotland and Wales. However, it's much hoped by Australian rugby union fans that the two teams will join forces in the near future, at which point the 'All Black Wallabies' will be the best in the world.*

Greg Norman

Greg Norman is a golfer who is nicknamed the Great White Shark because, just like those fearsome creatures, he has never won the US Masters, Open or PGA Championships.

---

*   It is reluctantly conceded that the All Blacks are already the best in the world.

A.B. 'Banjo' Paterson

Andrew Barton 'Banjo' Paterson, CBE (17 February 1864–5 February 1941) was an Australian bush poet, journalist and author. He in no way resembled a musical instrument. Rather, he used the name as a pseudonym in *The Bulletin*, so as not to threaten his concurrent career as a lawyer in the city.

Paterson's more notable poems include 'Waltzing Matilda', 'The Man from Snowy River', 'Clancy of the Overflow' and 'Please Don't Call Me Banjo, It Was Just A Pseudonym'.

Biography

Andrew Barton Paterson was born at a rural property near Orange, New South Wales, and grew up near Yass. Like many of the nation's most beloved producers of sentimental works of art about the Australian bush, he spent much of his adult life as far away from it as possible—mostly in Sydney, and also during several long periods as a foreign correspondent and soldier.

Paterson became a solicitor after failing his university admission exam, as, in those days, the smartest members of society were expected to do something more edifying than sorting out legal squabbles.

From 1885, Paterson began submitting poems to *The Bulletin*, which decided to publish them because he was white, and it had a burden to uphold*. His

---

*   In 1886, *The Bulletin* began using the banner 'Australia for the White Man'. It kept it until 1961, which is appalling until one recalls that the White Australia policy existed in some form until 1978, making them seem progressive for dropping it so early.

pseudonym, 'The Banjo', was a tribute to his favourite horse, leading to a defamation suit after it became embarrassed because people assumed it had composed Paterson's poems.

At the turn of the century, Paterson became a war correspondent, reporting from the Second Boer War in South Africa and the Boxer Rebellion in China. He subsequently abandoned his career as an eyewitness reporter at the heart of momentous world events in order to write whimsical poems about sheep.

As a city solicitor, this is about as bush as Paterson got.

Paterson served with distinction in World War I, ultimately rising to the rank of major, despite having been a household name in Australia for 20 years at the time of enlisting. But in spite of repeatedly travelling the world back when it was difficult to do so, and writing several novels, many short stories and extensive works of journalism, including many dispatches from several wars of enormous historical significance, 'Banjo' Paterson is best remembered for a handful of quaint early ballads commemorating the bush where he spent so little of his life.

Consequently, Paterson has long been considered Australia's national poet, and was universally admired across the nation until 2008, when his poem 'Waltzing Matilda' was performed in concert by André Rieu.

Best-known poems

'Waltzing Matilda'—Australia's national song describes the situation that led to European colonisation, a starving person stealing to feed themselves, in a fresh Australian setting. In its plot, an itinerant steals a sheep, is caught by a vengeful farmer, and commits suicide to avoid punishment at the hands of the troopers. 'Matilda' affirms that anyone who wants to resist the control of the wealthiest members of Australian society can do so only by becoming a larrikin ghost. It also reflects Australia's British priorities, as even those in reduced circumstances are able to enjoy tea.

'Mulga Bill's Bicycle'—a warning that cycling is a dangerous pursuit for vainglorious idiots. This poem predicted the folly of hipsters riding fixies decades before they became the scourge of our inner cities.

'The Man from Snowy River'—in which a valuable horse wants to run free with the wild brumbies, but is ultimately caught and brought back. A warning against nonconformity.

'The Man from Ironbark'—traces the origins of the hipster beard in Australia back to one cruel barber's practical joke.

'Clancy of the Overflow'—a city office worker romanticises the life of a shearer, while patronising his semi-illiterate friend, an actual shearer. A thinly disguised metaphor for Paterson's own career.

Pavlova

Pavlova, or **Aussie Delight**, is an Australian dessert, made by Australians, for Australians, in Australia. That fact doesn't change whether it is ultimately proven to have originated in Australia, or in that part of Australia known as New Zealand.

Pavlova is made of crisp, crunchy meringue on the outside and soft, gooey meringue on the inside, and whipped cream and fresh fruit on top, and is the best. The dessert is named after the Russian ballerina Anna Pavlova, who was, like her namesake, light skinned, very sweet, and often wore hats trimmed with strawberries and passionfruit.

The nationality of pavlova has long been disputed by those who assert New Zealand's independent identity, but the origin has not been definitively determined, with so much cultural interchange between the similar cookbooks of the relevant period that the debate ultimately demonstrates yet again that it's simpler to treat them as a single country, Australia.

Recent research has suggested that the dish may, in fact, have originated in America, and been an adaptation of a German dish, illustrating why it's often wise not to ask too many questions about where delicious desserts come from, and just believe that they're Australian.

In any event, pavlova is indisputably as Australian as the Anzacs, the Southern Cross, and health problems created by the excess consumption of sugar and cream.

Recipe

Beat Australian-laid egg whites to a stiff consistency, then fold in caster sugar from Queensland, gourmet vinegar from South Australia and corn-flour made from real Western Australian corn. Slow bake the mixture in a non-Fisher & Paykel oven while singing 'Waltzing Matilda'. Bake until the third quarter siren in an AFL game and then allow to cool. Top with cream from patriotic Aussie cows, and fresh fruit from a country that, unlike New Zealand, has tropics. Do not, under any circumstances, decorate with kiwifruit.

World's largest pavlova

In recent years, various New Zealanders have attempted to set a world record for pavlova. A 'pavzilla' was created in 1999, and in 2010, a 50-square-metre version with the Bledisloe Cup in the centre was created as a charity fundraiser. It should be noted that while admirable, these efforts don't mean that New Zealand gets to win the argument, because, in keeping with Australia's long tradition of Big Things, the town of Marulan in New South Wales once had a Big Pavlova.

Besides, in many respects, the world's largest pavlova is the one in all Australians' hearts.

Platypus

The **platypus** (*Ornithorhynchus anatinus*), is sometimes referred to as the **duck-billed platypus**. Because when the first species was sent to England, scientists thought it was a fake sewn together from bits of other animals, it's also known as **Frankenstein's Monotreme**.

Along with the echidna, the platypus is one of the few mammals that lay eggs instead of giving birth, and is also venomous, a rare quality it only shares with parking meter attendants and Mark Latham. The male platypus has a spur on its hind foot that delivers a poison that can cause severe pain to humans, particularly biologists who laugh at it for looking like it's been sewn together.

Monotremes are also unique among mammals for their electroreception ability, and the platypus has a well-developed capacity to sense the electric fields of any mammal, although it cannot pick up SBS. Platypuses tend to close their eyes, ears and throat when diving, which makes them uniquely suited to dumpster diving.

The platypus is generally nocturnal, except for those species in the Sydney region, which have struggled in recent years to find anything happening after dark. They have also been lost entirely from South Australia, having relocated to Victoria in search of more opportunities.

Like many Australians, platypuses eat 20 per cent of their body weight every day, but unlike the humans who do this, they need to do so to survive, and are able to burn off the energy.

The animal was used as a symbol of two of the daggiest events in Australian history—the Sydney 2000 Olympic Games and Expo '88. Despite this, biologists maintain that platypuses are in no danger of becoming extinct.

Poker machines

Poker machines, commonly referred to as the diminutive **pokies** out of misplaced affection, are as ubiquitous in Australian pubs as bad cover bands, ATMs with obscene surcharges and regulars with alcoholism.

They were previously known as **one-armed bandits**; however, due to changes in their design, this term is now an anachronism, because they no longer have an arm, not because they've stopped robbing punters.

Despite the name, they bear little resemblance to the game of poker except in that they're also a means of rapidly losing money.

History

Poker machines were first legalised by New South Wales in 1956, when they were placed in RSL clubs, to thank those who fought for their country by giving them the chance to lose the money they'd earned doing so. They also appeared in other registered clubs, as a means of assisting them in achieving their social benefits in an extremely antisocial manner.

Pokies were later made available in all pubs after the government deemed that venues where patrons consume beverages that reduce their capacity for reason and increase their impulsiveness were the perfect location in which to place gambling machines.

By 1999, New South Wales had roughly 10 per cent of the world's gaming machines, according to the Productivity Commission, a statistic that caused much shock across Australia. As a result, other state governments were inspired to catch up. A few years later, governments nationwide were earning several billion dollars a year from pokies, making them the ideal bodies to regulate gaming machines.

Pokie saloons are often labelled 'VIP Lounge', to the great confusion of visiting celebrities. *Ken Yae Wong*

Present day

Pokies are now available for use across much of Australia, except Western Australia, which coincidentally has a two-thirds lower rate of problem gambling.

Following innovations in game and machine design,

poker machines are arguably the only computer-related field in which Australia now leads the world. The leading Australian manufacturer, Aristocrat, has been particularly successful at helping many thousands of Australians join the underclass.*

There is now approximately one poker machine per 100 people in Australia, and in recent years the industry itself has begun to acknowledge that there is a significant gambling problem in society. However, they see the problem as stemming entirely from the widespread availability of offshore internet gambling, which they want to be more tightly regulated, lest it continue to lure away their customers.

Prime minister of Australia

The **Prime Minister of the Commonwealth of Australia**, also known as the **PM** or **Whoever's Running Things This Month**, is the head of government in Australia.

The PM is chosen by either their party colleagues or maverick crossbenchers to serve a term of two to three years before being dumped by those same party colleagues, on the basis of poor polling.

The public are also theoretically able to choose and remove their own leaders through the elections that are usually held every three years.

---

* Just so Aristocrat can't earn even more money from a defamation suit, the Productivity Commission estimated in 2010 that there were 115,000 problem gamblers across Australia, while Aristocrat recently became the world's largest poker machine manufacturer, so, clearly, many thousands of problem gamblers have played their machines. It's a real Aussie success story, except for most of its customers.

But this archaic approach has largely been discarded in recent years in favour of sudden assassinations, allowing voters to constantly hire and fire new leaders through the opinion poll process without the inconvenience of a nationwide ballot. Though this has led to substantial job instability for prime ministers, it has provided continuing employment opportunities for pollsters.

The job of prime minister is not mentioned in the constitution of Australia, which was intended to be a document that set down the Australian political system for future generations. The founders, in their wisdom, envisaged that voters would one day want to dump not just the incumbent, but the entire office of prime minister. Experts feel that the day is fast approaching.

Appointment

Though technically commissioned by the governor-general, prime ministers are, in fact, chosen by their colleagues on the basis of complex, self-interested deals, either before the party is elected to office, or suddenly, late at night, after it has.

This is because while technically a prime minister's most sacred duty is defending the nation, in practice their biggest priority is defending their colleagues' seats in parliament.

Prime ministers notionally serve up to three years before facing an election, although since 2010, the practice has been to deny all prime ministers the chance to face re-election, hoping instead that voters might feel more sympathetic towards someone who hasn't disappointed them in the intervening years.

Powers

The prime minister has extensive power across nearly all areas of government, until they do not. The schism between the text of the constitution and accepted practice has created a constitutional duel—both the prime minister and governor-general have the effective ability to sack one another, which is a charming customary hangover from the Westminster system except when it becomes a hopeless debacle, as in 1975.

Sir Edmund Barton, first prime minister and near-impossible trivia question.

Consequently, a prime minister can be sacked by their colleagues; the governor-general; the High Court; the Australian people, in the event of an election; and even the opposition, if it has the numbers to block supply. Combining this situation with Australia's notorious tall poppy syndrome, it's extraordinary that the nation's politics is as stable as they are at present—that is, stable enough to make Fiji seem immutable by comparison.

Privileges of office

The PM is the most senior and respected politician in the country, unless the office is held by a woman, in which case the public feels free to call her by her first name and make constant insulting comments about her appearance.

Residences

There are two official prime ministerial residences. In Canberra, the Lodge has long been the primary residence of Australian leaders, unless their personal unpopularity leads the staff to organise a lengthy renovation to coincide with their expected incumbency, in which case the prime minister in question resides in a police college.

In Sydney, the prime minister resides at Kirribilli House, unless they personally own a superior harbourside mansion. Some PMs make Kirribilli House their primary residence, in the event of having children at a private school up the road. The governor-general's residence, Admiralty House, is next door, allowing convenient access whenever one wishes to sack the other.

Vehicle

Previously, PMs travelled in armoured Holden Statesmans, but in recent years they have shifted to an equally Australian brand of car, BMW. The prime ministerial numberplate is always 'C1'—denoting 'Commonwealth', although some have suggested other words.

After office

Prime ministers are usually granted an office, staff, and travel within Australia. However, it has been suggested that this be revised, on the basis that the constant changes of prime minister are likely to send the Commonwealth bankrupt.

Significant prime ministers

Sir Edmund Barton (1901–03)—the first prime minister, but gave it away after two years to become a founding High Court justice, as that job is much harder to lose.

Sir Alfred Deakin (1903–04, 1905–08, 1909–10)—the member for Ballaraat,* and elected prime minister three times. Deakin created the Royal Australian Navy and purchased battleships, thus setting up the South Australian economy to be pork barrelled for decades to come.

Curiously, he once advocated for the White Australia policy by arguing that if Japanese people were allowed into Australia, they'd have an unfair advantage because they'd work much harder than white people. This is one of the few occasions in our political history when a leader has made a racist argument whose premise is inferiority.

Andrew Fisher (1908–09, 1910–13, 1914–15)—both the second Labour prime minister and the first Labor one, as the spelling was changed in 1912, and still hasn't been changed back. Having been PM for four years and 10 months in total, he's the second-longest-serving Labo(u)r PM after

Fisher, pictured here in 1899, could easily be mistaken for a Melbourne bartender in 2017.

---

* Not a typo, unless you accept my theory that the original spelling was a typo that nobody bothered to fix until 1977, when it changed to 'Ballarat'.

Bob Hawke, reflecting the party's extremely poor capacity to retain elected office and prime ministers.

Fisher also had the best moustache of any Australian PM.

Billy Hughes (1915–23)—Australian politics' ultimate chameleon, he was expelled from three different parties, and ultimately transitioned all the way from Labor to Liberal, a path only subsequently undertaken by Mark Latham.

Hughes is remembered as the leader who guided Australia through World War I, helped found the League of Nations, and died at 90 while still an MP, on account of having no hobbies. His many legacies include the formation of the Australian Federal Police, which was created in the hope that they might be able to stop the members of public throwing eggs at prime ministers, specifically himself.

Stanley Bruce (1923–29)—the most Melburnian leader ever, his middle name was Melbourne, he had a seat on the outskirts of the city, and he was later Lord Bruce of Melbourne. Consequently, he was the only Australian prime minister to have advanced barista skills, and also never to have visited, or even acknowledged, Sydney.

Like Kevin Rudd, he might have become UN secretary-general; unlike Kevin Rudd, his protestations of lack of interest were genuine.

James Scullin (1929–32)—became prime minister two days before the Wall Street crash that signalled the start of the Great Depression. He tried to implement Keynesian solutions, but was blocked, and the austerity measures he was forced to adopt instead were wildly unpopular, causing him to be voted out of office. Scullin's preferred approach was later adopted, with great success, by subsequent governments faced with economic crises, notably Rudd. This was no help to Scullin whatsoever.

Ben Chifley (1945–49)—a reformer with an extensive legacy in public housing, education and social services, Chifley famously described Labor's mission of building a social welfare state as the 'light on the hill'. This light was subsequently extinguished during the Hawke–Keating period.

Harold Holt (1966–67)—generally recognised as Australian political history's wettest Liberal.*

John McEwen (1967–68)—the last National or Country Party leader to serve as PM. He remained so for less than a month, after which the experiment was never repeated, despite, and also because of, Sir Joh Bjelke-Petersen's ill-fated attempt to move to Canberra.

John Gorton (1968–71)—the first prime minister whose middle name, Grey, was also an adjective.† Also the only prime minister to take the office from the Senate until Penny Wong tires of her colleagues' inadequacies and does so as well.

William McMahon (1971–72)—long considered the Coalition's least effective prime minister, until the arrival of Tony Abbott made it debatable.

---

* If this seems in poor taste, consider that it is in rather better taste than naming a swimming pool complex after him, as has been done in Glen Iris, Melbourne.

† His dull reputation was somewhat belied by the Ainsley Gotto affair, except that, Gorton being Gorton, this probably wasn't actually an affair. In fact, she was apparently having a relationship with Gough Whitlam's chief of staff at the time, a cross-party liason that was a far more unusual occurrence than an elderly boss having a fling with an underling.

Malcolm Fraser (1975–83)—the last liberal Liberal prime minister of Australia, Fraser is remembered for his role in the Dismissal, for which he subsequently atoned towards the end of his life by moving even further left than Whitlam.

Despite his hard-line attitude to his predecessor, Fraser was known as an extremely warm person, evidenced both in his welcoming attitude towards Vietnamese boat people, and his view that it was too hot to bother wearing trousers in warm climes.

Paul Keating (1991–96)—a genius when it came to financial reform, Keating was widely considered to be the best treasurer Australia ever had, except by Peter Costello. On his watch, the government floated the dollar, liberalised the tax system, reduced tariffs, deregulated banking and oversaw the shift to enterprise bargaining.

Was also prime minister.

Kevin Rudd (2007–10, 2013)—Kevin Rudd was famous for his apology to the Stolen Generations, and for not apologising for his efforts to undermine Julia Gillard's subsequent period as prime minister. He successfully navigated Australia through the global financial crisis with a series of bold, visionary decisions, and then took Australia into a local political crisis because of his subsequent meandering indecisiveness.

Some superstitious Canberra figures have suggested that after he was dumped by his colleagues, he cursed the office of prime minister such that no successor could stay in it for longer than three years—however, if so, it appears that, due to a lack of foresight, the curse also applied to Rudd himself.

Rudd will nevertheless be remembered as one of the most popular leaders in recent Australian political history, except with his colleagues.

Julia Gillard (2010–13)—the first woman to become prime minister, and probably the last for some time, given the reaction to her gender. Predictably, Gillard was mercilessly attacked by the right-wing commentariat; unpredictably, her appearance was also mocked by Germaine Greer. Gillard was the first prime minister never to have been married, and also the first to argue against marriage equality on the basis of her sincere belief in the traditions of an institution she and her partner had never bothered to pursue.

Gillard passed a record volume of legislation despite being in minority government, but was nevertheless dumped by her colleagues just before the election. This made her the most recent prime minister to both arrive in and leave office via a leadership spill.[*]

Gough Whitlam (1972–75)—A groundbreaking leader whose bold 'crash or crash through' philosophy was definitively resolved in 1975 in favour of 'crash'.

Property prices

The only thing worth talking about. Also the only thing talked about.

---

[*] At time of writing.

Qantas

Qantas, originally **Queensland and Northern Territory Aerial Services**, is Australia's oldest airline, although it is now flying to other places as well, and no longer promising 'service' in its name.

Nowadays, nearly a century after it began, Qantas is still proud to take Australians anywhere in the world they want to go as long, as Emirates flies there from Dubai.

The airline is every Australian schoolchild's proof that words starting with a 'q' don't always take a 'u'.

History

The airline was founded to provide a mail service in rural Queensland in 1920, and conducted the first flight of the Royal Flying Doctor Service of Australia in 1928. However, Qantas concluded soon afterwards that there was more money to be made flying well-heeled business travellers than assisting during medical emergencies.

It's rumoured that there is a Qantas Founders Outback Museum in Longreach, which catalogues these early days in rural Queensland, but it's not clear whether anyone has actually visited it.

Qantas began international services in 1935, flying to Singapore, which even then boasted the world's largest duty-free mall. It extended its reach to London from 1958, and since that time, has always had the Sydney to London 'kangaroo route' as its flagship service, driven by the constant desire of Australians to escape their isolation—for nearly 60 years, Qantas has been the official airline of Australia's cultural cringe.

Despite Qantas's longtime slogan, it's generally agreed that the spirit of
Australia is Bundy rum. *Terence Ong*

The airline has also profited extensively from the desire of Britons to
escape their weather.

In 1947, the Labor government nationalised Qantas, as was the fashion
in those naïve times of belief in public ownership. It remained under
government control until 1993, when it was privatised, as was the fashion
until 9/11 devastated the international passenger aviation market. Qantas
remains quaintly privately owned, and, even more quaintly in the modern
airline industry, recently returned to profit.

The Sydney to Melbourne route continues to be one of the world's busiest
and a major source of income for the airline, as Sydneysiders love to visit
Melbourne to shop, and Melburnians grudgingly visit Sydney for work, or
to confirm that it's as bad as they'd always been told.

In 1998, Qantas co-founded the oneworld alliance, then one of two global
airline alliances. After many years of marketing the reach of this global

network, Qantas largely abandoned it in 2013 for a one partner alliance with Emirates that meant its European flights now go through Dubai. However Qantas recently announced that it will be returning to Singapore for stopovers from 2018, after realising that its customers preferred visiting tiny authoritarian shopping malls that also offered a casino.

Qantas began flying the A380 in 2008, and was one of the first airlines to do so. Though at first it was hoped that the A380 would allow Qantas to boost profitability by squeezing more passengers onto each flight, the dramatic increase in the weight of the average Australian in the past few decades means that an A380 can now carry fewer Australian adults than used to fit on a 747.

In 2011, Qantas reacted to the prolonged industrial unrest that followed its failed union negotiations by boldly grounding its entire fleet. This inconvenienced approximately 68,000 passengers— a small price to pay for Qantas to bully its workers into submission. This move helped return the airline to profitability, as its passengers realised that the only thing worse than having to fly Qantas was not being able to fly Qantas because its flights were all cancelled.

In Australia, Qantas's market leadership has remained so strong that even the airline's long association with John Travolta has been unable to undermine its position.

Distinctive characteristics

For many years, Qantas has featured Indigenous artworks on some of its jets. This allows visitors to get a taste of Australia's unique Aboriginal culture without needing to engage with it meaningfully during their visit.

Qantas's ads have long featured a children's choir singing 'I Still Call Australia Home' by Peter Allen. This campaign, one of Australia's best known, is not only endearing to audiences, but allows Qantas to pay its performers less than it would if they were grown up, a clever cost-saving method that gave the airline a useful cost-cutting idea for Jetstar.

The Qantas Club is the airline's network of lounges around Australia and major international centres, which allow well-heeled passengers to associate with other irritating people. The clubs are known for their insistence on rigorous dress standards, and lax attitude to their self-service bars, which becomes particularly useful when flights are delayed.

There is also an invitation-only Chairman's Lounge.*

Famously, Qantas has never had a crash involving a jet airliner, winning the approval of fictional character Rain Man, although it did have some fatal incidents before 1945, meaning that technically, Rain Man was wrong.

So, and one wouldn't want to jinx this, Qantas has absolutely never had a crash involving a jet airliner. *Ever.*

Jetstar

In 2004, Qantas responded to the success of Virgin Blue by launching its own low-cost arm. With a logo depicting a single orange star, representing a rating out of five, Jetstar expanded on its parent's long reputation for service, comfort and reliability by showing that it could also manage a division that offered none of those things.

---

* Which the author will not joke about just in case he's ever invited to join.

Jetstar also expanded the 'leisure' market with cheap flights to Phuket and Bali. These routes proved very popular with the kinds of people who start drinking heavily in the terminal before boarding their flight, and the decision to charge these customers per beer, rather than following the all-inclusive approach customary on Qantas's own flights, led to the immediate profitability of the entire Qantas Group.

In response to Jetstar's success, Virgin Australia (as it was later known) took over Tigerair, showing that quality standards in Australian aviation had slipped so much that its previously 'budget' flights could now seem upmarket next to Tiger's. The key differential was that Tiger cost less than any alternative, and added an exciting gambling-style element to the trip, as there was no way of knowing whether your flight would depart on the scheduled day.

Jetstar now has low-cost subsidiaries around the region, including in Singapore, Vietnam and Japan. The gradual relocating of the Qantas Group's crews and servicing operations to cheaper hubs throughout the region has meant that, in the future, it will most likely only be Qantas's children's choir that truthfully calls Australia home.

Queensland

Queensland is the second-largest state in Australia, stretching from the extraordinary natural beauty of the Cape York Peninsula to the north, to the very ordinary developer-made ugliness of the Gold Coast.

The state is split into two distinct regions—North Queensland, the sparsely populated rural area whose major exports are sugar and idiosyncratic political mavericks; and the densely populated, urbanised south-eastern corridor that isn't proper Queensland, because there are too many hipsters and too few box jellyfish.

Nevertheless, the entire state is definitely more Queensland than the rest of Australia, a fact celebrated by the famous state war cry of 'QueenslandARRRRR!'*—growled to convey the state's famous larrikin character, a threat of impending physical harm, and that if the speaker hasn't downed a few XXXXs already, they're definitely just about to.

Queensland is famous for its natural beauty—in particular, the Great Barrier Reef, to which tourists flock in glass-bottomed boats to examine how rapidly a natural wonderland can be ruined by global warming. Visitors also enjoy Queensland's many iconic tropical destinations for their glorious beaches, friendly locals and permissive attitude to binge drinking.

The state was named by Queen Victoria, and while the southern state that bears her name was given it as a compliment to her, the decision to name Queensland was more of a case of Victoria complimenting herself by forging an association with what any Queenslander will tell you is the only good bit of Australia.

Queenslanders are often known as 'banana benders,' which is a ridiculous nickname, as recent shortages have made bananas far too valuable to interfere with.

From the broadness of its people's accents to the bizarre narrowness of their railway tracks, Queensland is just that little bit different. The locals wouldn't have it any other way—which is more a reflection of their stubbornness than it is of Queensland's superlative qualities.

---

* In some cases, the final syllable may constitute a subconscious cry for help.

Politics

Queensland is known for its strong culture of political independents, who tend to either flame out in the course of one term; stay around for decades to pass their seat on to their progeny; or win one term, go to prison, spend 20 years trying and failing to return, and then lead their party to four Senate seats.

Unusually for a political system derived from the UK's Westminster traditions, Queensland's parliament is unicameral, having dumped its Legislative Council after the political mavericks of the day convinced the public that the 'Upper House' had tickets on itself. This has allowed Queenslanders' preferred authoritarian leaders to unleash their bullying without the inconvenience of checks and balances.

Though nowadays it is constituted along more democratic lines, Queensland's parliament was once elected by an innovative gerrymandering system that belied the state's reputation for being traditional and hidebound. So skewed was the electoral system that the agrarian despot Sir Joh Bjelke-Petersen was able to remain in power for decades.

Undisturbed by his increasing unpopularity with a majority of Queenslanders, the peanut farmer turned premier continued to deliver his vision of a Brisbane where heritage buildings were demolished in the middle of the night, and freeways were built through pristine natural environments, and even the Brisbane River's northern bank. Citizens were relieved of the inconvenience of dissenting by a vindictive police force whose Special Branch victimised anyone who protested against anything, including the ban on protests. The skewed electoral system made Joh impossible to remove until the stench of corruption became so great that he lost even under the gerrymandered system.

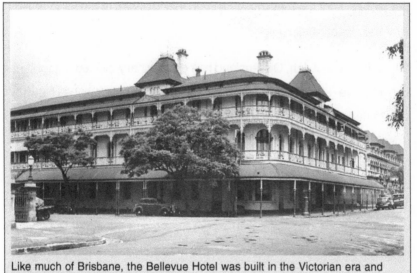

Like much of Brisbane, the Bellevue Hotel was built in the Victorian era and destroyed by Joh Bjelke-Peterson.

Under the National Party's electoral system, electorate sizes were determined by the 'Queenslandness' of each area, meaning that rural electorates had more voters than those in the inner city. To their credit, many country Queenslanders were uncomfortable with this system—although their solution was for the south-east of the state not to vote at all.

There are still proposals to implement a more permanent version of this plan by splitting North Queensland into its own state, permitting the 'real Queensland' to govern itself without having to defer to the inconveniently populous built-up areas of the south-east.

This would allow northerners to reflect their greater degree of Queenslanditude by founding the world's first maverickocracy, where political parties would be banned and any politician whose policy platform displayed internal cohesion would immediately be dumped from office. When it was pointed out to them that this proposal would give North Queensland an unfairly high number of seats in the Senate relative to its population, the architects of the movement claimed this was one of the main reasons why they wanted to do it.

Since the days of Joh, Queensland has occasionally elected authoritarian conservative governments again, most recently that of Campbell Newman, who gutted the public service so effectively that he made himself redundant from his own job after only one term.

The state's longest-running political debate has been over daylight saving. The south-east wants to introduce it, so as to share a timezone with the rest of the eastern states, with whom its thriving economy is so vitally linked; the farmers object because of some incomprehensible reason involving fading curtains. As ever in Queensland politics, the rural types prevail, as the state is, in many respects, more than one hour behind the southern states.

Despite its long conservative heritage, Queensland is the only state to elect two female premiers, illustrating the state's distinctive version of equality, where the only thing that matters in evaluating anybody is whether they're a Queenslander.

Sport

Identity

Queensland sport is irretrievably linked with maroon, and, to be even more specific, the exact shade of the bruises that the state's team inflicts on the NSW State of Origin team in rugby league's most prestigious annual contest.

Despite the accuracy of doing so, referring to the state's designated sporting colour as 'purple' is considered the height of rudeness. Queenslanders also don't appreciate outsiders describing their various jerseys as 'red-wine colour', as Queenslanders drink only beer. This is true to the extent that many domestic homes have modified their kitchen taps so that they offer only XXXX and XXXX Gold.*

State of Origin

Queensland's rugby league representatives are the most Queenslander of all Queenslanders, bringing honour upon their state with their habitual triumph in an intense contest that only matters in two states of Australia, despite regularly being played in a third.

The Maroons are the Harlem Globetrotters to NSW's Washington Generals, except with the obvious difference that basketball is a popular international sport. The Maroons, at least if you ask a local, have won the annual Origin contest every year, including those before it was first held. In the same way, every native Queenslander is a winner because the state of their origin is Queensland.

It's an axiom of the contest that the Maroons will always make a successful comeback in any State of Origin game, except when they let NSW win the first of the three-game series, as a means of twisting the knife even further.†

The greatest Origin player of all time is Wally Lewis, known as 'the King' because Queensland will gladly do whatever he says. Mal Meninga is also a very popular figure, due to an extraordinary set of accomplishments in the field of torturing Queensland's southern neighbour, including repeatedly winning Origin as captain, winning Origin as coach even more

---

* This is a slight exaggeration—nobody would drink XXXX Gold.

† This line was written before the 2017 series. (Sigh.)

often, and winning a string of NSWRL premierships for Canberra that humiliated every club in NSW.

He's also known for running for political office for only 28 seconds—the perfect length for a political career.

When it comes to the Maroons, Queenslanders are more open-minded than they're given credit for, having turned out in droves to vote for Glenn Lazarus's Senate campaign with the Palmer United Party. Even though he played Origin for NSW, his string of premierships with Maroons' feeder team (and maroon wearers themselves) the Brisbane Broncos was enough to activate his adopted state's trademark parochialism.

Note that 'Maroons' is pronounced to rhyme with 'owns' in Queensland— a helpful mnemonic is to think of the moans emitted by NSW fans throughout each game.

NRL

The Brisbane Broncos were the first Queensland team to join the NSW Rugby League before their competition went national. Their colour scheme builds on the state's preferred maroon one, combining it with the distinctively gold colour that's symbolic of the sun, beer, sugarcane, sand and the money the team's owner, News Limited, injected into the game during the Super League war, tearing it apart.

The Broncos are the only team owned outright by a media company that also broadcasts games and prints newspapers, ensuring an extraordinary consistency in how the team is covered across most forms of popular media.

Once, the Broncos were supported throughout the state—now, there is a hotly contested Queensland derby between the Broncos and the North Queensland Cowboys, unless, of course, either team is playing southerners. Despite the rivalry, both teams have some elements in common, like copying their names from well-known American football franchises.

The Cowboys' most iconic player is Johnathan Thurston, a man so pre-destined to excel in rugby league that his parents spelled his first name with two 'H's, symbolising the two uprights at either end of the field. Thurston previously played for Melbourne, a fact that has done nothing to reduce his popularity with Queenslanders, as the Storm play in purple jerseys and have a common interest in seeing NSW lose.

Rugby union

The Queensland Reds, the state's Super Rugby team, chose their name because they, too, slightly resemble the Maroons. While at first rugby union was a tough sell in league-mad Queensland, people soon realised that the competition gave them even more chances to see NSW beaten at football, so the Reds have won considerable support in recent years.

AFL

The Brisbane Lions have become a credible force in the game, famously winning three premierships in the early 2000s, leading to ambiguous feelings for their old fans from Fitzroy. The one-time Brisbane Bears' position of providing comic relief for the code has now been taken over by the new Gold Coast Suns.

Cricket

The Queensland Bulls were well known for decades as the team that had never managed to win the Sheffield Shield. After they finally managed to do so, the Bulls had no remaining distinguishing features.

Brisbane

The state capital is known to the locals as 'Brisvegas', presumably ironic-ally, since it contains Australia's tiniest casino. But the city has a number of things in common with Vegas, like its instant approval of any building project, no matter how farcical.

Brisbane also shares Las Vegas's quality of being a place that's great to visit for two or three days, but being there any longer will start to undermine your hold on reality.

As it's Australia's only city with a pleasant year-round climate,* Brisbane would be a genuinely enjoyable place to live were it not overrun with Queenslanders. While its watering holes tend to be enormous barns of places with decor inspired by 1980s airport lounges, recent years have seen the development of a number of fashionable areas like Red Hill and Fortitude Valley, but that doesn't mean you aren't a solid chance of getting glassed if you go drinking in them.

The city's favourite annual event, 'Riverfire', takes place during the Brisbane Festival, and involves a fighter plane dumping fuel along the central section of the river and then lighting it. Every year so far, the city has survived, but crowds continue to turn up to watch, just in case.

Major Queensland tourist attractions

Australia Zoo—a family business run by the Irwin family for several
generations, the zoo's mission is to protect endangered species, and
raise money to do so by endangering humans.

---

* Sorry Darwin, you're too hot to qualify.

Warner Bros. Movie World—it's like Hollywood on the Gold Coast, both in the sense of celebrating movies and of being a glib, shallow, money-obsessed region that should probably be bulldozed immediately.

Sunshine Coast—a bit like the Gold Coast on a more constrained budget.

Brisbane Beach—a pile of sand plonked on the south bank of the Brisbane River. Reminiscent of the city's endless construction sites, it makes visitors yearn for Queensland's many spectacular natural beaches.

Magnetic Island—sounds like it should be part of the Bermuda Triangle, but has far fewer attractions than a regular magnet.

Kuranda—an extraordinary pristine rainforest that visitors may briefly glimpse beyond their thousands of fellow tourists.

Byron Bay—not only is it a lovely beach town with a cool alternative vibe and some of the country's top music festivals, but it has the added benefit of being just over the NSW border.

Racial Discrimination Act

The controversial section 18C of the Act is a restriction on free speech, and has also limited political speech in another sense, as many media organisations seem to view 18C as the only topic worth talking about.

Yahoo Serious

The Australian actor, writer and director **Yahoo Serious** really did change his name from Greg Pead to Yahoo Serious. He didn't adopt it as a pseudonym—he legally, bindingly changed his name to Yahoo Serious.

Serious is best known for the film *Young Einstein*, which explores what might have happened if Albert Einstein had been a Tasmanian apple farmer who had figured out how to split the atom with a chisel in order to put bubbles in beer, inventing rock 'n' roll, saving Paris from an atomic bomb and falling in love with Marie Curie along the way. It has taken certain liberties with Einstein's biography.

His subsequent films imagined Ned Kelly in the Hollywood film industry, and the Sydney Opera House as an egg factory that, on account of a dastardly plot, produced nicotine-laced eggs, flights of ahistorical whimsy which proved considerably less charming to audiences.

Serious once tried to sue Yahoo!, but couldn't prove that the internet company was preventing him making money under the name 'Yahoo'.*

Yahoo Serious's oeuvre represents peak quirk in the Australian film industry, so much so that, unlike a Serious film, none of the above facts have needed to be exaggerated.

It is unknown whether anyone is making a quirky film about his life that takes considerable liberties with its facts, but someone should.

Sledging

Sledging is a sporting technique where, as described by master practitioner Steve Waugh, witty jokes are made in order to induce temporary 'mental disintegration' in one's opponents.

---

* Rather, it was the plot of his subsequent movies that was to blame.

It's a normal part of proper traditional cricket as it's played in Australia, but has been subjected to unfair and unjustified criticism that's nothing like the good-natured banter Australians wearing the baggy green direct at their mates on the other team out in the middle.

Usage

The objective of sledging is to disrupt a player's concentration. Playing well requires constant focus and discipline, which can be considerably more difficult if one's opponents, to cite a random example that definitely didn't happen, are making the sounds of a steam locomotive at an incoming bowler who lost his sister in a train accident.*

Sledging is a core skill within Australian cricket, as crucial as batting, bowling and fielding. Those who don't indulge in it, like Adam Gilchrist, might be respected by their peers for their principled goody two-shoes stance, but will never truly be part of the team, and probably don't even drink all that much, either.

From their earliest days of learning the game, young Australian cricketers are taught to find opponents' weaknesses and exploit them through barbed comments. An opposing player's body shape, ethnic background, personal circumstances, life history—anything is grist for the sledging mill. It's common for school cricket players, for instance, to make unflattering taunts about a player's mum. In later years, that will change to taunts about their wife, and after their retirement, their daughters—it's all part of the circle of sporting life.

---

* It is unclear whether this happened, but if not, the fact that someone thought of it, even as a rumour, is still appalling.

The best players will find a way to respond, either with the bat, ball or their own mouth. Everyone else simply isn't good enough for the top level, and will be told so.

Sledging teammates

One of the most famous sledges in Australian history was a case of 'friendly fire', when it was said of bowler Scott Muller in his second Test in Hobart that he 'can't bowl, and can't throw'. Much of the debate centred around the identity of the accuser, with Shane Warne accused, before 'Joe the Cameraman' from Channel Nine subsequently confessed.

Muller never played for his country again, meaning that it was the selectors who delivered the ultimate sledge.

Socceroos

The **Socceroos** are the Australian men's association football team. They have enjoyed considerable success in recent years, to the point where the only truly embarrassing thing about them is their nickname.

The team is known for its hard-tackling, intensely physical style, which is a polite way of saying that they do not possess much finesse when passing or dribbling.

The Socceroos' second-greatest success in their long and patchy history came when they won the Asian Cup at home in Sydney in 2015. But their greatest triumph occurred in 2005, when they convinced FIFA to let them transfer from the minnow-filled Oceania confederation to Asia, making their path to World Cup qualification significantly easier.

Ever since, the team have shown their true potential by making the World Cup finals each time,* but winning only two of the 10 games they've played.

The team's 'golden generation', who qualified for the 2006 Cup the hard way against Uruguay, also featured stalwart goalkeeper Mark Schwarzer, a recognised penalty specialist, who became one because of the team's constant habit of conceding them; and Mark Viduka, a striker with a

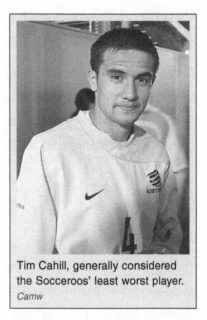

Tim Cahill, generally considered the Socceroos' least worst player.
Camw

fine scoring record when not playing for the Socceroos. Striker Tim Cahill is still playing for the team, making him more of a golden oldie.

The team is currently captained by Mile Jedinak, whose fame within the broader Australian community is such that former PM Tony Abbott accidentally called him 'Mike'.

It's widely hoped within the Australian football community that the national team will someday be taken seriously in the world game, but it's not sufficiently widely admitted that this will never happen while they're called 'the Socceroos'.†

---

* As of the time of writing, this record was in major jeopardy.

† The Matildas, Australia's women's national team, have been more successful internationally, and are currently ranked in the top ten teams by FIFA. However, in keeping with the Australian game's funding priorities, they don't warrant any more than a footnote in this book.

Snugglepot and Cuddlepie

Tales of Snugglepot and Cuddlepie is the first in a series of well-known children's books written by May Gibbs, which has won considerable fame within the field of children's literature for giving the cloying cuteness that is traditional in the genre a distinctively Australian setting.

Characters

The two titular characters are 'gumnut babies' of uncertain taxonomical status, who blend elements of human babies and cherubs, and dress in items swiped from gum trees. They are generally depicted in Gibbs's own drawings in states of near-total undress with various leaves and pods draped around them, making May Gibbs the Anne Geddes of her day,

Given their resistance to clothing, it seems somewhat implausible that Snugglepot (or is it Cuddlepie?) would wear pads.

except that she didn't subject actual children to her vegetation-based indignities.

One baby is called Snugglepot and the other Cuddlepie, and they are so indistinguishable that had the book been reviewed by a competent management consultant before publication, Gibbs would undoubtedly have featured only one character, Snugglepie. The two babies' greatest ambition is to meet a human, in what is the least plausible element of Gibbs's story.

Mr Lizard is their dear friend and sidekick. He is, in fact, a goanna, and would it have killed May Gibbs to be more specific?

There are also various female characters whose names begin with 'little', even though the first of them, Little Ragged Blossom, is the same size as Snugglepot and Cuddlepie. She has somehow obtained proper clothes from the natural environment, unlike her loincloth-sporting friends, but never shares her source with them.

Little Obelia is the other one, although she should probably be called Littler Obelia, as, at one point, Little Ragged Blossom goes and cares for her under the sea, because, naturally, underwater childcare is exclusively the domain of a female character—despite May Gibbs being a working woman herself.

The antagonists of the series are Wicked Mrs Snake, whose identity doesn't exactly have many shades of grey, and the Big Bad Banksia Men—ditto. While Gibbs's use of one of the more unusual items in the rich treasury of Australian flora is highly creative, the way she draws them is a bit—at the risk of retrospectively destroying many an Australian childhood—racist. Whereas the 'good' Gumnut Baby characters all have rosy-pink skin.

Other minor characters in subsequent instalments of Gibbs's series include Chucklebud and Wunkydoo, Nuttybub, Nittersing and Narnywo,* and Bib and Bub, all of whom represent an unsuccessful attempt to get lightning to strike twice in the same place. It would be genuinely challenging to differentiate any of these characters from Snugglepot and Cuddlepie in a gumnut police lineup.

Legacy

In recent years, attempts have been made to continue the series with the original characters, a significantly better idea than Gibbs's continual attempts to invent new, less good characters, but one that arrived decades too late. Clearly, *Snugglepot and Cuddlepie's Sleepover*, which depicts the two original heroes under a leaf blanket with Little Ragged Blossom parked in between them, represents a considerably more modern take on the characters than in Gibbs's original.

Gibbs's work is destined to remain an important chapter in the history of Australian children's literature, both because of her innovative repurposing of Australian flora and fauna as characters, and because the racial tensions that make the Banksia Men so problematic still haven't been resolved nearly 100 years after she first began telling these stories.

Mr Squiggle

Mr Squiggle is the star of an eponymous Australian children's television program about a puppet from the moon who draws upside-down pictures

---

* Which sound like I've just made them up as a parody, but are actually quite real.

with his nose. This premise was sufficient to entertain Australian children for 40 years.

The show's producers sought contributions of simple line drawings from their show's young viewers. They were then ruined by Mr Squiggle, who turned them into less creatively abstract representations of familiar every-day items and situations, completely undermining the integrity of the original artwork. It is also unclear how he had such a broad knowledge of Planet Earth's variety of subject matter, leading some viewers to doubt whether he even really hailed from the moon, especially since he never shared his advanced commuter rocket technology with the earthlings who welcomed his weekly visits.

The lunar alien–artist was aided and abetted in this mass defacement of children's original artworks by a range of human assistants, who were themselves changed every few years. It's thought that the woman who notoriously destroyed a precious 19th-century Spanish fresco* by painting a crude face on its surface was inspired by watching Mr Squiggle.

The program contributed to the negative stereotype of artists as scatter-brained and erratic, as Squiggle would often get distracted and go for what were incorrectly termed 'space walks', even though he remained subject to the Earth's gravity throughout. As a result, millions of Australians who grew up watching Mr Squiggle struggle with physics to this day.

Mr Squiggle ultimately left our screens because its creator, Norman Hetherington, who had operated and voiced all the puppets throughout that entire period, refused to let anybody else near his creation. This was because among the many positive values the program promoted to its audience of children, sharing was nowhere to be found.

---

* *Ecce Homo*, by Elias Garcia Martinez, later 'improved' by Cecilia Giménez.

Friends and associates

Blackboard—constantly urges Squiggle to 'hurry up', despite his name, appearance, and entire purpose in life being for people to draw on him, and despite evidently having nothing better to do with his time, as he appeared alongside the 'man from the moon' for 40 years. Also, while he resembles a blackboard of the sort that used to appear in children's classrooms, he is, in fact, an easel.

Gus the Snail—in many ways the antagonist of the show, perhaps because its creators replaced the shell that served as his home and protection with a television, and later a flower pot, sacrificing his domestic comfort for a visual gag.

Bill Steamshovel—loves corny jokes, but never considers the intriguing riddle of why he appears in the show, seeing as he has nothing to do with the kids' drawings that are the reason for watching it. Had the program been broadcast by today's ABC, Bill would have been subjected to a redundancy.

Swimming in Australia

Swimming rivals cricket as Australia's national sport, both because of our proud history of champions, and because in convict times it was the best means of escape from the penal colonies.

Our connection with the sport runs so deep that the most effective stroke, the front crawl, was originally known as the Australian crawl, as it resembles the crawl through a gutter that is so commonly a feature of an Australian night out. Continuing this deep association, the band

Australian Crawl had a frontman, James Reyne, who slurred his words when singing.

Australia's long history of success in swimming also reflects the fact that it's one of the few Olympic sports where pasty white people have a chance of winning medals.

Australia's national swimming team is known as the Dolphins, after the more Australian alternative, the Dugongs, was rejected by unimaginative sponsors. Despite the opportunity to offer a moving tribute, the Holts also failed to win much support as a nickname.

Famous swimmers

Dawn Fraser—one of three swimmers to win the same event at three Olympics in a row (100 metre freestyle) and the only one ever to be denied the chance to go for a fourth because she stole a flag. Also, the only Australian of the Year to get in trouble because of a lark during the year of their reign.

Ian Thorpe—the most successful athlete in Australia's Olympic history, he experienced extraordinary success during his swimming career, except when it came to deflecting

Dawn Fraser. It's not clear whether there is a flag concealed in this bag. *Noske, J.D. / Anefo*

inappropriate and intrusive questions about his sexuality.

Shane Gould—a teenage prodigy, she was the only Australian ever to win three individual gold medals in the same Olympics, and also the only Australian ever to give up the sport shortly after doing so.

Lorraine Crapp—was, in fact, a fine swimmer, the first woman to swim the 400 metres in less than five minutes.

In the water, Ian Thorpe often intimidated other swimmers thanks to his unique hair fin. *Xiaming*

Susie O'Neill—a dual gold medallist, she was nicknamed 'Madame Butterfly' after her American husband abandoned her in Japan.

Kieren Perkins—a renowned long-distance swimmer, his first name is often misspelled; generally Keiran, Kieran, Kearan, Keeran, Keeren, Khiran, Kihyearhayn or Kirin Beer.

Murray Rose—while fondly remembered by some Australians for winning three gold medals at the 1956 Melbourne Olympics, he is more famous for his appearance in the Rock Hudson movie *Ice Station Zebra.**

Hayley Lewis—became a superstar in Australia in 1990, when she won five gold medals at the Auckland Commonwealth Games at the age of 15. She only managed a silver and a bronze in Olympic competition, leading to the fierce Australian determination to protect the Commonwealth Games from being abolished on account of their obvious irrelevancy. She later became a host of *The Biggest Loser*, which had absolutely nothing to do with her inability to win Olympic gold.

---

* This may not be correct, but is worth it to mention *Ice Station Zebra*.

Sydney Opera House

The **Sydney Opera House** is one of the world's most famous and iconic buildings, and Australia's most significant cultural landmark. Designed by the Danish genius Jørn Utzon, it's one of the country's most-visited tourist attractions, used throughout the year for concerts, plays and ballets; and even outdoor concerts, when the residents of nearby apartments aren't able to put a stop to them.

The only minor shortcoming with the Sydney Opera House, if one insists on nitpicking, is that, due to various disputes throughout its construction, its Joan Sutherland Theatre is completely inadequate for staging major operas. But, otherwise, a lovely building.

Austen Tayshus

His single 'Australiana' is the best-selling single in Australian history, which is too much for a koala to bear.

Television in Australia

Australian television formally began in Sydney on 16 September 1956, roughly 20 years after the UK and 15 years after the US. That interval between the various markets has been maintained ever since.

Channel Nine was the first station on air, setting an all-time ratings record of 100 per cent of the Australian television audience. Nine would never manage this lofty peak again, however, which makes a regrettable exaggeration of its long-term slogan, 'Still the One'.

The initial Channel Nine broadcast featured a dinner-suit-clad Bruce Gyngell saying, 'Good evening, and welcome to television,' followed immediately by an infomercial for a product known as the Ab-matic.

Shortly afterwards, Channel Seven became the first station to broadcast to Victoria, and its black-and-white transmissions quickly proved an ideal match for Melbourne's monochromatic wardrobes. Barry Humphries featured on the first day of broadcasts as his character Mrs Everage, who at that time was mistaken by the majority of viewers for a genuine Melbourne housewife.

Nine and Seven, followed by the ABC, had opened their stations in time for the beginning of the Melbourne Olympics on 22 November, and the broadcasts were immediately popular with the nascent television audience, who found themselves consistently cheering for the grey team.

The Menzies government had announced in 1954 that Australia would adopt a two-tiered system, with two commercial broadcasters and a government channel under the auspices of the then Australian Broadcasting Commission. Despite having created it, the Liberal Party would never support ABC TV again.

During its early days, videotape technology was in its infancy, so most programs were broadcast live to air. The ability to play programming from overseas decimated local production, both because imported programming is generally cheaper than making local programs and because local audiences hadn't realised how shoddy most Australian shows were until they could compare them with imports from the UK or US.

Bruce Gyngell welcomes viewers to television—the only dignified moment in the medium's history.

Much earlier programming involved musical variety and quiz programs, adapting formats that had been popular on radio. As time passed, however, television became dominated by drama and current affairs, while Australian radio gravitated towards furious opinions and childish pranks.

Over the coming years, television would spread across Australia's state capitals and then its regional centres. This led to a flowering of local production and talent across the country, which was abruptly halted by coaxial cable links that allowed programming to be networked from Sydney and Melbourne and for the smaller state and regional capitals to be ignored, as is standard today.

Australia's third commercial broadcaster was launched in 1964. Adopting the number 10 in some parts of the country and 0 in others, it soon

became known as the 0/10 network, an accurate reflection of the quality of its early programming. Nowadays, it is simply known as the Ten
Network, an accurate reflection of the quality of its current programming
if scored out of 100.

Nevertheless, more interesting local programs were slowly beginning to be
produced—notably the drama series *Homicide* and live variety programs,
including *In Melbourne Tonight*, which took Melbourne's constant boasting
about its nightlife to a national stage for the first time.

Satellite arrives

The first satellite telecast to Australia took place from Expo 67 in
Montreal. Prime Minister Harold Holt opened the Australian Pavilion,
which showcased events including boomerang throwing, sheepdog trials,
woodchopping contests, and a concert by artists including Normie Rowe,
The Seekers and Rolf Harris. It was the first time that such advanced
technology had been used to beam something so fundamentally trivial
across the globe. While the circumstances of Harold Holt's subsequent
disappearance remain mysterious, it's sometimes postulated that shame
at his involvement in this event is one of the reasons for it.

Australia participated in the first global satellite hookup two weeks later,
on 25 June 1967, for an event called *Our World*. Fourteen countries
took part, each showcasing a significant aspect of their culture. The UK
provided the Beatles debuting 'All You Need Is Love' live from Abbey
Road, while Australia chose to reflect the rich cultural life of this young,
ambitious nation by broadcasting a Melbourne tram leaving its depot.*

---

* If you don't find this story (which actually happened) amusing, congratulations on
living your whole life in Melbourne.

The colour era

Test broadcasting in colour began from 1967, but the full changeover did not occur until 1975, enabling the full effect of Norman Gunston's garish suit to be seen in the nation's living rooms during the Dismissal.

Much of the rush to purchase colour sets was driven by an increase in live sports broadcasting. Sport has continued to drive technical innovation in Australian television today, although its commentary teams remain resolutely Neanderthal.

The country's second national broadcaster, the Special Broadcasting Service, took over the unacclaimed Channel 0 identity from Ten after its launch in 1980. Aimed at the multicultural population, SBS also won many fans from the non-multicultural populace, who enjoyed its programming of soccer matches, and movies with high levels of arty nudity, which has been proven by the network to entirely transcend any cultural or language barriers.

The next expansion followed the launch of community television in 1994, leading to the philosophical question of whether a channel with no viewers can really be considered a channel at all. This maxim was later explored by some of the programming on Sky News, which arrived around the same time, with the advent of subscription television.

Early pay TV providers included Galaxy, Foxtel, Optus and Austar, or, as they're known in today's more diverse media market, Foxtel.

The arrival of pay television sparked the Super League war, during which News Limited and Channel Nine split the code in half, providing one inferior competition for each network. A truce was achieved after both sides belatedly realised that they'd almost destroyed the game.

2000s to today

The Seven Network's broadcast of the Sydney Olympics set ratings records, as viewers flocked to the combination of live sport and parochialism that has always proven popular with Australian audiences.

Digital television arrived at the same time, offering both multi-channelling and high definition to free-to-air broadcasters. To date, these channels have largely been used for high-definition repeats of low-definition programs.

The arrival of high-quality, high-definition broadcasting in the Australian market has proven that, despite the exciting opportunities to showcase the best programming from around the world, in what is being described as the golden age of television, the medium in Australia will always be dominated by crappy, low-budget imports.

In the past year or two, streaming services have proliferated, meaning that watching television no longer even requires a television or a network of transmission towers. The relentless march of technology threatens the Australian television industry as we know it, which is obviously a good thing.

Popular commercial television shows

Home and Away—the story of an angry, ginger-headed entrepreneur called Alf Stewart, who battles a series of flaming mongrels to 'Make Summer Bay Great Again'.

Blankety Blanks—game show where comic-genius presenter Graham Kennedy says 'blank' in lieu of various dirty words. Lost its appeal by the time all the words were allowed to be said on television.

Number 96—1970s raunchy soap set in an inner-city apartment block. The choice of a number that is '69' backwards was surely not a coincidence.

60 Minutes—enough current affairs to fill exactly 47 minutes.

Prisoner—set in a women's prison, this drama series is still one of the only Australian TV series to have a predominantly female cast. It became hugely successful around the world, which led the nation's television producers not to try any more female-led shows again for decades.

Young Talent Time—a program pairing talented kids, some of whom went on to become international stars, with an older man with extensive industry experience who served as a type of mentor and father figure. Johnny Young, whose surname made the show's title a typically cheesy pun, closed each show by singing 'All My Loving' to the kids as they gathered around him. There is absolutely no way this program, and especially that ending, could exist today.

The Price Is Right—a long-running quiz program where contestants had to guess the price of various things. Nobody ever guessed just how cheap this thing was to make.

Here's Humphrey—a long-running program on Channel Nine, *Here's Humphrey* was always compromised by budget issues that made it impossible to employ a voice actor, or even purchase trousers for the loveable but silent and semi-naked bear.

Fat Cat and Friends—a similar program on Channel Seven, back when Seven's programming felt like a low-rating knockoff of Nine's hits, rather than the other way around, as is the case today.

Australia's Funniest Home Video Show—a valid claim solely because it was Australia's only home video show.* For 25 years this stalwart

---

* Well, except for *Australia's Naughtiest Home Video Show*, the Doug Mulray-hosted program which suffered *broadcastus interruptus* after a phone call from Kerry Packer.

combined wacky sound effects with amateur footage of horrifying injuries. It's generally best forgotten that it was initially hosted by a late-career Graham Kennedy.

Blue Heelers—a hugely popular drama that showcased the young Lisa McCune's dogged four-year hold on the Gold Logie.

Hey Dad..!—a long-running sitcom that isn't funny anymore for both on- and off-screen reasons.

Healthy, Wealthy and Wise—a program most famous for introducing Australia to celebrity chef Iain 'Huey' Hewitson, who certainly didn't appear to fit the first adjective in the title of the program. As one of the first lifestyle shows on Australian TV, this superficially cheerful program has a chilling legacy.

Skippy The Bush Kangaroo—the most expensive program ever produced in Australia at the time of its premiere in 1968, at $6000 an episode, none of which was devoted to varying the scripts.

'What's that, Skip? Kangaroos can't actually make clicking sounds?'

Telstra

Telstra Corporation Limited, formerly known as **Telecom Australia** and informally known as **Bloody Telstra**, is Australia's largest telecommunications provider. Formerly a government-owned monopoly, it now combines the slow, unresponsive, monolithic approach it took in public ownership with premium pricing. It is, however, highly innovative in developing new charges.

In many remote parts of this large, sparsely populated continent, Telstra is the best choice for consumers, because it is the only choice.

Successive governments' inability to sensibly plan and maintain an advanced national broadband network has not only made a strong argument for privatisation, but has achieved the improbable effect of making Telstra seem well managed by comparison.

Divisions

Copper network

Telstra still owns the cables that connect much of the country to the regular telephone network, guaranteeing the company a steady stream of revenue for the next few decades until everyone who cares about having a landline or thinks that ADSL offers a sufficiently rapid internet connection* has passed away.

---

*   That is, the nation's grandparents.

Mobile network

Telstra has always offered the highest-quality network at the most expensive price, and its recent decision to reduce its fees from unbelievably expensive to merely extortionate has won it considerable market share, assisted by the self-immolation of Vodafone. In recent years, several high-profile outages have led numerous customers to leave Telstra, until they try the competition's coverage and come straight back.

Broadband network

This has been a successful division, despite the indefensible decision to name it 'BigPond'. Telstra is frequently in a position to offer consumers the fastest connection because of its cable TV network, and Australians' determination to pay a premium for high-quality internet access so they can pirate movies for free has proven a reliable source of customers.

Foxtel

Telstra partnered with News Corporation to set up Australia's only pay television provider. News brought its extensive programming library and expertise to the table, while Telstra provided its long experience in operating a monopoly.

Directories and advertising

Telstra's directory offshoot, Sensis, was once very profitable, due to the popular *Yellow Pages* directory that was an indispensable item in every Australian home. Its function of being the first place people search for the businesses and services they need has successfully been transferred online, albeit to Google.

Future

Telstra is likely to experience dramatic change down the track, as all of its legacy services move onto the internet, and overseas providers begin connecting Australians via new wireless offerings, but it's hard to pin down when this will occur. Best estimate is that it will probably take place between seven and twelve years in the future, and it won't call in advance.

Payphone banks like these were once spread across Australia, and it was occasionally possible to find one that hadn't been vandalised. *Maksym Kozlenko*

Thongs

The Australian **thong** is a variety of sandal that unites a slab of foam rubber with a strap that passes between the big and second toes. They are known as flip-flops in other parts of the world, but in Australia that term is used exclusively in politics.

Thongs are lightweight, cheap to purchase, and are both waterproof and capable of floating. They are generally considered to be the least glamorous items of clothing ever invented by the human race, with the possible exception of lederhosen.

Not to be confused with the underwear also known as the G-string, thongs first arrived in the West from Japan, where GIs had adapted them from the local *zori* sandals. However, thongs are constantly confused with G-strings by visitors to Australia, to the general amusement of all, and embarrassment of those shopping at stores that sell both items.

The thong's Japanese origins should not be seen as making them any less iconically Australian. Even Australia's flag is predominantly imported—the important question is how Australian something feels, which in the case of thongs is 100 per cent. Furthermore, thongs decorated with the Australian flag are available, and represent the theoretical maximum of Australianness.

Another sense in which thongs are is distinctively Australian is that they are generally manufactured overseas.

Thongs are the perfect garment for Australian life, in that they are highly casual; suitable for the beach; and easily detached from the foot, whereupon they can be thrown, either in an athletic competition traditionally conducted in pubs, or at somebody.

They can also be used for slapping crocodiles, although this is not generally recommended as an effective deterrent.

While the thong protects Australians against hot sand, broken glass, tinea and not being considered a legend, some podiatrists have warned against this form of footwear, due to the propensity of wearers to injure their feet because of design flaws inherent in the thong. The British estimate that, in 2010, thong-related injuries cost the National Health Service £40 million. However, when considering that statistic, it should be borne in mind that all those surveyed were British.

The thong is likely to remain the footwear that most Australians don for their most important journeys, such as heading down the servo for a Chiko Roll and some cigs.

Malcolm Turnbull

Malcolm Bligh[*] **Turnbull** was the 29th prime minister of the Commonwealth of Australia, from 15 September 2015 until his replacement by _____ on _____, 2017.

Two-up

Two-up is a simple betting game developed by Australian soldiers in the trenches of World War I. Playing it allows contemporary Australians to understand that, along with the mortal peril the Anzac soldiers faced in that bloody conflict, many troops were waging a protracted conflict against boredom.

Rules

A 'spinner' takes two pennies and throws them in the air while players bet on whether they will fall both heads, both tails or 'odds'. That's it.

---

[*] If naming your child, consider not naming them after someone who experienced two mutinies against his leadership, just in case they ever become prime minister or opposition leader and it becomes ironic. Then again, Malcolms are known for ruthlessly seeing off their political opponents.

'Come in spinner!' is always called at the start of play, even though it's redundant, as they're in the trench right next to you.

History

It's believed that the game was first developed after the troops finally tired of 'I Spy', to which the only possible answers in that era were 'trench', 'more trench', 'even more trench' and 'incoming mortar'.

The original version of two-up, known as 'one-up', was popular for a time, but the addition of the second coin gave the game lasting appeal. One would-be innovator attempted to popularise 'three-up', arguing that the extra coin would lead to more possibilities and therefore a more mathematically interesting contest, but he was punched by a fellow soldier for being a nerd.

Role in modern society

Two-up is traditionally played on Anzac Day, especially after those marking the occasion have consumed enough beer to forget how interesting they found the game the last time they played it.

In some areas, the game is legal to play only on Anzac Day. This is so that it won't lose its appeal unless players also find themselves engaged in protracted trench warfare.

Two-up was originally available at Star City Casino in Sydney (now The Star) in a nod to Australian tradition, but it was abandoned in 2003, after management belatedly realised that there was no way for the house to make its usual profits out of a game with genuinely equal odds.

Successors

Having proved that Australians will bet on literally anything, two-up has been succeeded by a multitude of other gambling contests, including horse, greyhound, snail, crab and cockroach racing, and elections, the latter being the only contest more demonstrably tedious than betting on coin tosses.

Uluru

Uluru, also known as **Ayers Rock**, or **Uluru/Ayers Rock** if you're the fence-sitting Northern Territory government, is a large sandstone rock formation in central Australia.

In the Pitjantjatjara language, the rock has been called 'Uluru' since time immemorial, but some surveyor named it after some bureaucrat in 1873, and since then, Sir Henry Ayers' name has proven impossible to shake from a UNESCO World Heritage Site where it's got no business being.

The Aṉangu traditional owners request that visitors not climb the rock, due to both its spiritual significance and their sense of responsibility for the safety of visitors. It can nevertheless be climbed, if you're the kind of person who would climb onto the altar at your local church.

Vegemite

A yeast paste first eaten as a dare by brewers who had consumed too much of their own product, **Vegemite** was subsequently deemed fit for human consumption by accident, following an error by regulators who thought they were approving it for use as an axle grease for heavy machinery.

The dark brown spread, made from leftover brewer's yeast that should have been thrown away, has since become an iconic Australian food, albeit one that still should be thrown away.

Perfectly decent toast ruined by Vegemite.
Tristanb

Vegemite's enduring success despite tasting like salty, rancid beer has been cited by nutritionists as proof that human beings will eat anything as long as there's enough salt in it.

History

Vegemite's development resulted from Marmite shortages during World War I. While this should have provided an opportunity for Australians to liberate themselves from their addiction to a foul-tasting dark brown paste that had been imported from Britain, along with their ancestors' stoic ability to neglect their tastebuds, Fred Walker & Co saw a business opportunity.

In 1919, one of its employees, Cyril Percy Callister, successfully blended rejected yeast from Melbourne's Carlton & United Breweries, where it had been deemed too unpleasant even for Foster's Lager, with salt, and extracts of celery, onion and mouldy socks, long essential ingredients in British cuisine.

The product was launched commercially in 1922, and a nationwide competition christened it with a name that was extremely similar to Marmite, but not quite legally actionable. While the company closely guards the recipe for Vegemite, it's safe to say that it contains little to no vegetables—the strongest connection arguably arises from the product being dirt-coloured.

When Marmite deliveries resumed, Vegemite sales dropped. In 1928, the Walkers renamed the product 'Parwill', to make use of the slogan 'Marmite but Parwill'. To the great surprise of the manufacturers, this pun failed to electrify the yeast spread market, and in 1935, the Walker company changed the name back to Vegemite. Sales remained tepid.

'Parwill' sounds like a bad joke rather than a real product—here's proof it was both.

Vegemite ultimately defeated its British foe after Walker established a partnership with J.L. Kraft & Bros to market their processed cheese. The popularity of 'Kraft Walker Cheese' led Fred Walker to promote his earlier product by providing coupons that enabled purchasers to receive a jar of Vegemite for free. The decision to offer the spread at its correct value of zero pounds led to a significant increase in its popularity.

Walker's willingness to try anything to foist Vegemite on the people of Australia also led him to launch poetry competitions where the winners could receive imported Pontiac cars. In response to its taste, 'Vegemite' was commonly rhymed with 'plight', 'fright', 'blight', and 'not as good as Marmite'.

Vegemite finally prevailed over Marmite after the onset of World War II, when the English product again became unavailable. The Australian knockoff was included in army rations and became hugely popular during wartime, when shortages meant that less foul-tasting products were unavailable.

In April 1984, a jar of Vegemite became the first product in Australia to be electronically scanned at a checkout. In the current era of self-scanning checkouts, consumers frequently steal the product, due to a deep, lingering belief that its true price should still be $0.

Vegemite was sold in New Zealand for over fifty years, but it is no longer produced there, due to a lack of popularity that is either due to it being associated with Australia, or New Zealand consumers not being blinded by patriotism, and therefore responding appropriately to its taste.

In January 2017, Bega Cheese concluded a deal to acquire the spread and once again bring it under Australian ownership. It will presumably once again be supplied free with cheese.

Consumption

The most common approach to consuming Vegemite is not to. In Australia, however, it's most commonly eaten on toast with a layer of butter to counter the taste. Vegemite sandwiches often feature cheese alongside the spread, as a throwback to the days when Australians only ate it because they'd got it as a freebie, so thought they might as well eat it, since it was supposed to have vitamin B in it, or something.

Lettuce, avocado and tomato are also commonly used to overwhelm the taste of Vegemite.

In recent years, the spread has been the subject of some controversy due to its halal certification, which has left ultranationalist bigots unsure whether to boycott it in protest, or eat even more of it because it's so despised by non-Australians.*

Marketing

The most famous advertisement for Vegemite began in 1954, with a trio singing about how they were 'happy little Vegemites' and enjoyed it for 'breakfast, lunch and tea', back when tea constituted a separate meal, which makes it sound more British than Australian.

This was one of the most deceptive ads ever aired in Australia, as even the most avid fan of the spread would not be able to endure it for three meals a day. The advertisement also aired in black and white, making it impossible to verify the claim that it 'puts a rose in every cheek'.

Nevertheless, this campaign successfully promoted the spread to children, and most Australians now grow up eating Vegemite. This has led them to normalise its repellent taste, and consider it a 'healthy' part of their diet. This culinary variant of Stockholm syndrome explains why nearly all Australians love their national spread, while any overseas visitors from countries other than the UK cannot understand how they can stomach it.

---

* The author is as Australian as, and hasn't liked it since he was a kid. Love it or leave it does not apply to Vegemite.

Variations

Having struck it lucky with one spread made from the foul-smelling byproducts of beer, Vegemite's manufacturers have tried to produce a range of related products. All have experienced difficulties in the marketplace, due to having a foul Vegemite-like taste, but not having been force-fed to children since they were too young to know better.

Vegemite Singles—a Vegemite flavoured Kraft Single slice, sold in the 1990s. This proved unpopular because people generally enjoy pairing Vegemite with cheese, as opposed to Kraft Singles.*

Vegemite Cheesybite—this pairing of Vegemite and cream cheese was initially marketed via a competition to find its name, the results of which were announced during the 2009 AFL grand final. The resulting name, 'iSnack 2.0', was the most amusing deliberately bad name proposed via any public competition until the advent of 'Boaty McBoatface'. The name was abandoned after four days, and replaced by the current name. Ever since, AFL commentators have argued about whether the 2009 grand final was lost by St Kilda or Vegemite.

My First Vegemite—an attempt to produce healthier, less horrible-tasting Vegemite for kids. It failed, because parents preferred to indoctrinate their children into their own full-strength habit, much as alcohol addiction frequently passes across generations.

Cadbury's Dairy Milk chocolate with Vegemite—yet another attempt by Kraft to mix Vegemite with one of its brands, this was a block of

---

* Just before anyone from Big Cheese calls their lawyer, the US FDA has determined that Singles do not qualify to be called 'pasteurised processed cheese'. Also bear in mind that during manufacturing, each slice is prepared individually, rather then being sliced from a block, as with cheese. In any case, due to complex ownership changes, Kraft Singles are now called something else entirely.

Caramello chocolate with added Vegemite. It tasted like you'd expect, and consequently is no longer sold.

Overseas reception

US president Barack Obama said it tasted 'horrible', and then, speaking on behalf of the Free World he led at the time, correctly described it as 'a quasi-vegetable by-product paste that you should under no circumstances smear on your toast for breakfast'.

It's unknown whether Donald Trump enjoys Vegemite, but because it's unpleasant and served in an ugly yellow-tinted package, many experts believe he would.

Visual arts in Australia

The first **Australian art** was created by Aboriginal painters on the walls of caves. Contemporary Indigenous painters are in great demand internationally, with the better-known artists' works commanding very high prices, a high proportion of which tends to go to unscrupulous non-Aboriginal dealers.

Early European artists attempted to capture the essence of a unique continent, to enable their compatriots back home to understand their new home, but all failed. Nowadays, Australian artists' works can be compared with the best from the Northern Hemisphere, although doing that makes them look less good.

One of the first identifiable groups within Australian painting, the Heidelberg School, had more success at portraying Australia. It was strongly influenced by European impressionism, even lifting the name of the movement from Europe. Heidelberg artists like Fred McCubbin and Tom Roberts attempted to capture the effects of the harsh Australian light for the first time, frequently while also depicting the harsh Australian social policies of the era.

The nation's most prestigious art event is the Archibald Prize for portraiture, held annually at the Art Gallery of New South Wales since 1921. Each year, the nation's most important painters submit a diverse range of fascinating entries, after which the trustees generally give the prize to a mate.

Today, Australia has a thriving art scene, with many important institutions across the country, from the cutting-edge Gallery of Modern Art in Brisbane to the prestigious National Gallery in Canberra. There is also, inexplicably, a 'National Gallery of Victoria'.*

Prominent Australian artists

Ken Done—Australia's most successful artist to have T-shirts as a major element of his practice, Done has painted the Sydney Harbour Bridge even more frequently than the people who paint the Sydney Harbour Bridge.

Pro Hart—though a successful artist known for his loose, expressive, figurative style, his most famous work was executed on carpet and destroyed immediately.

Rolf Harris—having once painted the Queen's portrait for a BBC series, this kangaroo has recently been very much tied down, sport.

---

* Some Victorians defend the name on the basis that the gallery was named in 1861, long before Federation. Having gone from being a colony to being a state, Victoria has never been a nation.

McCubbin's 'On The Wallaby Track' reassured gallery visitors that even families with nothing still had tea.

Tom Roberts—known for taking the outback and the shearer's shed and placing them on gallery walls for people who'd never dream of leaving the inner city to experience them personally.

Grace Cossington Smith—famously painted Australia's first post-impressionist painting, *The Sock Knitter*, and also its first post-post impressionist painting, *The Sock's Finished Now*.

Charles Blackman—renowned for dreamlike images often imbued with a sense of foreboding, and also for his decades spent providing the voice of Dickie Knee on *Hey Hey It's Saturday*.

Margaret Preston—one of our earliest and most renowned modernists, she primarily chose to explore how the rapid change she saw in contemporary society affected vases of flowers.

Arthur Boyd—known for transposing Biblical scenes to contemporary Australia, as in his renowned portrayals of Noah and his tinnie, David spear-tackling Goliath in an NRL game, and Jesus turning water into VB at his local RSL club.

Fred Williams—Australia's finest landscape painter working only in the medium of polka dots.

Brett Whiteley—a highly successful painter who, in 1978, won all three of the Art Gallery of New South Wales's annual prizes, the Archibald, the Wynne and the Sulman, and was never forgiven for it by the rest of the art establishment, the precocious jerk.

Mike Parr—an internationally renowned performance artist, Parr once had his arm nailed to a wall for 30 hours, in a potent representation of the pain involved in watching much performance art.

Albert Namatjira—a highly successful landscape painter, Namatjira was evidence that an Aboriginal man could be welcomed into European society, as long as he had exceptional talent at an art form valued by Europeans. He and his wife were the first Aboriginal people from the Northern Territory to be released from being wards of the state, which allowed him to vote and is a reminder that, yes, every other Aboriginal person in the Northern Territory was legally treated as a literal child in 1950s Australia. Namatjira's relatively kind treatment abruptly expired when he was locked up under dubious circumstances, and he died soon after his release, so they got him in the end, regardless.

Shane Warne

Shane Keith Warne, better known as **Warnie**, is a former Australian legspin bowler and current international playboy. He is considered one of the worst best cricketers of all time.

Lauded for his prodigious performance on and off the field, Warne was a Wisden Cricketer of the Year in 1994, Vodafone's Text Messenger of the Year in 2004 and Diuretics Australia's Ambassador-at-Large in 2003.

Warne's first Test for Australia was the 1992 New Year's match against India at the Sydney Cricket Ground, and his most recent test was as a contestant on *I'm A Celebrity . . . Get Me Out Of Here*. He lost to Brendan Fevola, but won, in that Fevola was raising money for the Shane Warne Foundation; but lost, because, by that time, the foundation had closed down in a storm of negative publicity.

During his career, Warne took 708 Test wickets, 293 one-day international wickets, and $5000 from an illegal bookmaker, 'John', in 1994.

Warne also scored more than 3000 runs, the most by any player without a Test century,* and also scored at a record rate off the field. As well as Australia, he represented Victoria, Hampshire, the Rajasthan Royals and the Melbourne Stars, all with great success, and Nicorette, less successfully.

Post-retirement, Warne has become a commentator, taking advantage of his prolific gifts in all forms of communication, and a professional poker player, having become addicted to high stakes while gambling on his marriage. Warne officially retired from all forms of cricket in 2013, but is yet to cease playing around.

Early football and cricket career

Shane Warne was born to Keith and Brigitte Warne on 13 September in a year Warne maintains is irrelevant, as 'You're only as young as the one you feel'. Schoolboy promise led to him joining the St Kilda Cricket Club, and then joining the St Kilda under 19 team. Though he made

---

* Warne's top score of 99 is arguably more distinctive than if he had accumulated a century—although it's not as though we needed a reminder that Warne is fallible.

the reserve team the following year, he was later delisted, after being deemed to have too much promise for a team dedicated to never winning the competition.

Warne never lost his love of the sport, however, and was later famously photographed hand-passing a ball to friends. The ball in question was attached to both another ball and a large inflatable penis, and the friends were female and had temporarily misplaced their clothes.

A rare photo of Warne not taken from Instagram or CCTV footage. *Tourism Victoria*

Having determined that Shane Warne was no Saint, he abandoned AFL and moved to the Australian Cricket Academy in Adelaide, where he continued to roll his arm over, and get his leg over.

International cricket career begins

Warne toured to Zimbabwe with Australia B, and went on his first tour to India, with Australia A, in December 1991, beginning a deep relationship with the country that continues to this day. Warne is on the record as saying he loves India's people, its culture, and the food he eats while travelling there, tinned spaghetti from Australia.

It was India that served as the opponent for Warne's first Test in January 1992, at the spin-friendly Sydney Cricket Ground. Warne played poorly, leading the crowds to ask for the first time a question that would dog him throughout his career—who ate all the pies? Warne inevitably refuses to answer, although he is willing to admit to eating all the tinned spaghetti.

After two lacklustre performances, he was dropped 'the one time that wasn't due to jealousy', as he puts it. Warne was recalled for the Melbourne Test, and got a match-winning 7/52 and all the pies he wanted.

In 1993, Warne marked his debut out of Australia, and his first Ashes series, by bowling the veteran Mike Gatting from a long way outside leg stump. It was one of the most substantial deviations Warne has ever achieved outside of his personal life, and was nicknamed the 'Ball of the Century'—the only time the latter word was ever used in relation to Warne's cricketing achievements.

The spinner went on to become a regular, and then essential, part of the team, as Australia moved to dominate the sport. His reputation grew, and so did Warne himself, passing the 300-wicket mark and the 90-kilogram mark in 1998.

After injury led to an extended absence, his understudy, Stuart MacGill, established himself in the team, taking 12 wickets to Warne's two after the latter returned at the SCG Test in 1999. MacGill took wickets at a faster rate than Warne for much of his career, and chalked up only slightly fewer wickets per Test than Warne, accumulating an excellent 208 across his 44 Tests. But Warne tended to be preferred whenever he was available—after all, MacGill preferred wine to beer.

In his prime, Warne was known for his extensive and effective range of deliveries beyond those of the standard legspinner. He had a huge range, from the topspinner; to the flipper; to the mysterious zooter; and, finally, the delivery that best reflected Warne's own personality—the wrong 'un.

On top of this extensive arsenal, Warne also regularly claimed to have developed various 'mystery balls' ahead of a crucial Test series, but experts tended to doubt this, citing the bowler's inability to keep any aspect of his life secret.

Vice-captain

On Mark Taylor's retirement in 1999, Warne was made vice-captain to Steve Waugh, given his expertise in the area of vices, but was dropped from the team shortly afterwards upon hitting a patch of poor form. Warne has yet to forgive Waugh for this inevitable response to his underperformance, despite the captain defending him the following year, when he was once again dropped from the vice-captaincy after sending text messages to an English nurse that displayed even poorer form.

Warne was replaced by Adam Gilchrist, who was so relentlessly uncontroversial that, despite being one of the most exciting openers in history, he somehow managed to be boring.

The legspin genius's chances of becoming captain ended for good in 2002, when Ricky Ponting was appointed captain of Australia's one-day squad, having only been involved in a handful of scandals, compared with Warne's dozens. While 'Punter' was known for his love of the track, he'd never wagered his whole career by providing reports to the local bookie.

After continuing his rapid accumulation of Test wickets, man of the match awards and tabloid front covers, Warne's continuing success was interrupted by a shoulder injury in December 2002, thought to be related to his constant habit of lifting schooners.

Warne bowling in the Big Bash League in 2011. Post-retirement, he has continued to attend big bashes whenever possible. *Chris Brown*

Ban for controlled substance

Shortly afterwards, he was banned for taking a 'fluid tablet', as he called it, to lose weight, a cause that immediately won public sympathy.

Though it was a banned substance, the public's long familiarity with Warne led most to conclude that the action was due to stupidity rather than cheating. His reputation for honesty was consequently not tarnished, while his reputation for getting himself into trouble remained roughly the same.

During his year of suspension, Warne began a commentary career, and served as an unpaid consultant to the St Kilda Football Club. Following his involvement, they won the pre-season cup on several occasions before falling short later in the season, following the classic early-flair-before-frustrating-failure approach that Warne so often used with the bat.

Warne also performed some community work during this period, raising public awareness of diuretics, their controversial use in weight loss, and their banned status in major sports including cricket.

Return to cricket

On his return, Warne resumed his wicket-taking contest with Muttiah Muralitharan. Though at times there was tension between the two legendary spinners, Warne ultimately cleared the air, saying that he was a 'great fan of dodgy action', and 'who among us hasn't chucked during a big night match'?

Warne took his 1000th wicket in international cricket in his final Test, becoming the second person to reach this landmark after Muralitharan, but the first to do so without being no-balled by an Australian umpire with a chip on his shoulder. On his retirement, Warne had a world-record 708 wickets, an impressive mark only beaten by Muralitharan, and a hypothetical Stuart MacGill with more opportunities.

After leaving representative cricket, Warne played Indian Premier League, finding the Twenty20 format perfect for a man with increasing girth and decreasing stamina. He captained the Rajasthan Royals for four years, winning a title in the first season of the competition. Under his leadership, the Royals became the first-ever Indian sports franchise to win a major competition while eating only tinned spaghetti and baked beans.

Personal life

Warne was married to Simone Callahan for 'much longer than I expec-ted', and their family includes four children—Brooke, Summer, Jackson and Shane himself. As with his cricket career, Warne made repeated comebacks in the relationship, only to be thwarted after errant text messages. Meanwhile, Callahan entered the public spotlight by appear-ing on *Dancing with the Stars* in 2006, only to exit it again shortly afterwards.

In 2010, there was footage of Warne kissing the actress Elizabeth Hurley, who has long been drawn to men who get into sex scandals. Warne and Hurley's relationship grew as the couple explored a shared interest in narcissism, and they were engaged a year later, but ultimately split in 2013, to pursue their self-interest separately.

Warne's current personal situation is unknown, but he's admitted to being on the dating app Tinder, so it's assumed that he's available. It's also assumed that even if he's in a relationship, he's probably still available.

Foundation

The cricketer set up the Shane Warne Foundation, to 'enrich the lives of seriously ill and underprivileged children'. While it claims to have distrib-uted millions of dollars to children in need, media reports suggest that the foundation has also enriched the lives of members of the Warne family, who were employed by and received rental income from it. After negative publicity and Consumer Affairs Victoria formally advising that it was considering deregistering the foundation, Warne shut it down and retired hurt from running his own charity.

Jessica Watson

Jessica Watson OAM (born 18 May 1993) is a young sailor who achieved worldwide fame after her remarkable solo voyage around the world at the age of 16, completed in 2010.

Watson serves as an inspiration to young people to follow their dreams, dare to achieve, and carefully check the rules lest they also spend 210 days at sea, facing dangerous waves and potentially life-threatening collisions, without ultimately setting a world record.

Despite not following an officially recognised route, undertaking a voyage that many yachting experts criticised as dangerous, and holding dual citizenship with New Zealand, Jessica Watson has been acclaimed as an Australian hero, and was named Young Australian of the Year by a grateful nation that was mostly just glad she finished her trip in Sydney rather than Auckland, and didn't die en route.

Really, really early life

When she was a young girl, Jessica Watson's family lived on board a 16-metre cabin cruiser for five years. She completed her education via distance learning, covering most regular aspects of a formal education, but learning not as much as she wanted to about suitable escape methods from tiny floating prisons.

When she was eleven, her mother read to the children, as a bedtime story, Jesse Martin's book about his solo circumnavigation of the world. Watson's initial reaction was that she was at least four years too old for bedtime stories, but because there was nowhere feasible to hide from her mother, she was forced to listen, and eventually started dreaming of her own solo journey.

Upon returning to dry land, Watson's parents suggested that she begin planning the trip as a distraction from her plan to prosecute them for the prior five years of imprisonment at sea.

Watson rounding the Cape of Good Hope, when she still had good hope of setting a world record. *Andrew Fraser*

One of Watson's test voyages was interrupted by a collision with the 63,000-tonne bulk carrier *Silver Yang* but, despite the utterly unambiguous message about the safety of her undertaking, she decided to persist. Being unable to avoid major obstacles would be the enduring theme of her voyage.

Successful non-circumnavigation

Watson's first problem was that sailing authorities had decided not to recognise under-18s records on policy grounds, fearing that if they did so, it would ultimately lead to toddlers perishing while attempting to try to sail around the world.

There has also been debate over whether Watson's route, mostly around the Southern Hemisphere with a brief jaunt across the equator, was long enough—Martin had previously sailed to two points opposite one another on the globe, achieving what has been recognised as a 'true' circum-navigation. Watson was deemed to have fallen short of this yardstick, on account of not entirely understanding what circumnavigation was.

Despite Watson not ultimately setting any recognised records, a large crowd showed up to welcome her to dry land at the Sydney Opera House, where she received a level of acclaim usually reserved for seals. Then-flailing prime minister Kevin Rudd greeted her with his usual folksy cheer, recognising a fellow traveller who set out to make history, yet would ultimately fall frustratingly short.

Nevertheless, Watson remains a popular figure, due to her bravery, and persistence in spite of poor weather, huge waves and terrible advice. Her boat, *Ella Baché's Riskiest Sponsorship Deal*, was ultimately bought by the Queensland Maritime Museum as an inspiration to young Queenslanders to consider leaving their home state.

Despite the debate over Watson's accomplishment, she remains the youngest person to nearly circumnavigate the globe but fall short thanks to bureaucratic intransigence and her team's lack of adequate preparation. Her voyage will long be remembered as almost an achievement for the ages.

The Wiggles

The Wiggles, also known as **The Skivvies**, **The Cockroaches** and **The Four Children's Entertainers of the Apocalypse**, are the world's biggest children's band.

Their massive success can be compared with AC/DC, if the children were in the audience instead of onstage, playing lead guitar in a weird school uniform.

Known for their monocolour clothing and monotonous music, and accompanied by such not-quite-copyright-infringing characters as Dorothy the Dinosaur, Wags the Dog and Captain Feathersword, The Wiggles have become the most widespread and widely feared Australian export since the Hendra virus.

In recent years, three of the band's original members have been replaced by younger reincarnations, in a process based on the Tibetan system for appointing the Dalai and Panchen Lamas. Consequently, the only hope of stopping this process from continuing indefinitely is Chinese government intervention.

The Wiggles now also franchise their music and image across the world, much like McDonald's, except more popular with kids, and even more unpopular with parents.

Origins

The Wiggles began as a group of misanthropic former kindergarten teachers. Inspired by the tale of the Pied Piper of Hamelin, they planned to wreak their revenge on parents for years of patronising remarks at drop-offs and parent–teacher nights by seducing a new generation of children with addictively repetitive music.

But while the Pied Piper took the children away from their parents, The Wiggles' far more devious plan was to leave them where they were, constantly demanding yet another play of the band's music until the parents were transformed into catatonic, drooling husks who were only capable of muttering the words 'Wiggly Woo'.

The Wiggles. *Anthony Arambula*

Educational value

While the band members are committed to children developing cognitive, linguistic and social skills via their music, and work with expert educators to achieve this, multiple studies show that the major development in children who have been exposed to The Wiggles is the desire for more Wiggles.

When children listen to The Wiggles, they learn about the four primary colours—red, yellow, blue and purple. They're taught that dogs, pirates and octopuses are not to be treated with caution but, rather, are special friends. And they learn that when someone is asleep, like Jeff or his successor, Lachy, the right thing to do is shout at them to wake them up.

It's this ritual interruption of their rare moments of sleep, even more than the endless repetition of 'Hot Potato!', that has caused many parents of Wiggles fans to be placed in rubber-lined rooms.

Members

The classic line-up is Anthony, Murray, Greg and Jeff—note that Wiggles don't have surnames. Following the retirement of three of the four original members, the current lineup is The One Old Guy Who Didn't Retire, The New Old Guy, The Goofy Looking Guy, and Emma Who Is A Girl. The latter two Wiggles are married to each other, but it's best not to tell kids about that.

The generational change has proven so successful that Emma is now the most famous Wiggle in Wiggly history. There is an Emma Army of young girls dressed in special Emma merchandise, such as yellow bows and dresses, which are available from all Wiggly retailers. A solo career cannot be far away, with the likely result that the Wiggles will split up at last. However, due to their highly successful franchising program across Asia and other parts of the world, the Wiggles are like a hydra, so removing one set will merely spawn more Wiggles to take their place.

All Wiggles are equal, but some are now more equal than others.
Eva Rinaldi

Hidden messages

While The Wiggles' image is child friendly and the band is only too keen to stress its educational credentials, many songs contain hidden messages that are potentially harmful to children.

Songs with problematic subtexts

'**Hot Potato**'—encourages kids to eat carbs of varying temperatures.

'**Toot Toot, Chugga Chugga, Big Red Car**'—glamourises drink-driving.

'**Can You Point Your Fingers and Do The Twist?**'—shames children with motion difficulties.

'**Get Ready To Wiggle**'—offers foreplay tips.

'**Wake Up Jeff!**'—encourages bullying of narcoleptics.

'**Uncle Noah's Ark**'—advocates creationism.

'**Shaky Shaky**'—mocks earthquake victims.

'**Here Comes a Bear**'—shames a gay subculture.

'**Do The Daddy Long Legs**'—teaches that playing with spiders is fun.

'**We Like To Say Hello**'—endorses interaction with strangers.

'**Crunchy Munchy Honey Cakes**'—promotes marijuana use.

For more, please consult Wikipedia,
and add your own jokes.